IMPERIAL GUARD

By Robin Cruddace

CONTENTS

Introduction 3

The Imperial Guard 5

The Hammer of the Emperor 6
Lord Solar Macharius 13
Famous Regiments of the Imperial Guard 14
Notable Battles of the Imperial Guard 22
A Galaxy at War 26

Forces of the Imperial Guard...........................29

Company Command Squad 30
Regimental Advisors...31
Commissars 32
Primaris Psykers...33
Techpriest Enginseers 34
Ministorum Priests 35
Platoon Command Squad 36
Infantry Squad 37
Heavy Weapons Squad 38
Chimera Armoured Carrier 39
Veterans 40
Penal Legion Troops 41
Ogryns 42
Ratlings 43
Rough Riders 44
Sentinels...45
Storm Troopers 46
Psyker Battle Squad 47
Leman Russ Battle Tank 48
Hellhound Flame Tank..50
Hydra Flak Tank 51
Ordnance Battery..52

Manticore Rocket Launcher..54
Deathstrike Missile Launcher 55
Valkyrie Assault Carrier 56
Lord Castellan Creed & Colour Sergeant Kell.................57
Knight Commander Pask 58
Sergeant Bastonne 59
Colonel 'Iron Hand' Straken 60
Guardsman Marbo..61
Gunnery Sergeant Harker 62
Commissar Yarrick 63
Captain Al'Rahem...64
Commander Chenkov 65
Mogul Kamir...66
Nork Deddog 67

Wargear 68

Weapons 68
Vehicle Armoury 70
Armour 71
Other Equipment 71

Soldiers of the Imperial Guard..........................72

Imperial Guard Army List 89

HQ...90
Elites 94
Troops 96
Dedicated Transports 99
Fast Attack...100
Heavy Support 102

Summary 104

Written by: Robin Cruddace.

Art: John Blanche, Alex Boyd, Robin Carey, Paul Dainton, David Gallagher, Neil Hodgson, Nuala Kinrade. **Book Design:** Carl Dafforn, Emma Parrington, Mark Raynor. **Editorial:** Graham Davey, Andrew Kenrick. **Photography:** Christian Byrne, Matthew Hutson, Jim Sowter, Stuart White. **Production & Reprographics:** Simon Burton, Chris Eggar, Marc Elliott, Kris Jaggers, John Michelbach, Melissa Roberts, Rachel Ryan, James Shardlow, Kris Shields, Ian Strickland, Madeleine Tighe. **Games Development:** Alessio Cavatore, Robin Cruddace, Graham Davey, Andy Hoare, Jervis Johnson, Phil Kelly, Jeremy Vetock, Matthew Ward. **Hobby Material:** David Andrews, Nick Bayton, Mark Jones, Chad Mierzwa, Chris Peach. **'Eavy Metal:** Fil Dunn, Neil Green, Darren Latham, Keith Robertson, Joe Tomaszewski, Anja Wettergren, Kirsten Williams. **Miniature Design:** Michael Anderson, Juan Diaz, Martin Footitt, Jes Goodwin, Colin Grayson, Mark Harrison, Alexander Hedström, Matt Holland, Neil Langdown, Alan Perry, Michael Perry, Ali Morrison, Trish Carden, Brian Nelson, Seb Perbet, Dale Stringer, David Thomas, Tom Walton, Jonny Ware. **Special thanks:** Stu Black, Alan Merrett, Rick Priestley, Tim Sawyer.

Produced by Games Workshop

UK	US	CANADA	AUSTRALIA	NORTHERN EUROPE
Games Workshop Ltd., Willow Rd, Lenton, Nottingham, NG7 2WS	Games Workshop Inc, 6711 Baymeadow Drive, Suite A, Glen Burnie, Maryland, 21060-6401	Games Workshop, 2679 Bristol Circle, Unit 3, Oakville, Ontario, L6H 6Z8	Games Workshop, 23 Liverpool Street, Ingleburn, NSW 2565	Games Workshop Ltd., Willow Rd, Lenton, Nottingham, NG7 2WS

INTRODUCTION

The Imperial Guard is the largest and most diverse fighting force in the entire galaxy. This Codex is the definitive guide to collecting and playing with an Imperial Guard army in the Warhammer 40,000 wargame.

THE WARHAMMER 40,000 GAME

The Warhammer 40,000 rulebook contains the rules you need to fight battles with your Citadel miniatures set in the war-torn universe of the 41st Millennium. Every army has its own Codex book that works with these rules, allowing you to turn your collection of miniatures into an organised force ready for your games of Warhammer 40,000. This Codex details everything you need to know about the Imperial Guard.

WHY COLLECT AN IMPERIAL GUARD ARMY?

The soldiers of the Imperial Guard are but normal men facing a galaxy of superhuman warriors and lethal alien predators. They rely on superior numbers, disciplined training and above all else, honest human courage. Of all the armies in the 41st Millennium it is the brave souls of the Imperial Guard with which it is most easy to identify with.

The Imperial Guard is an army that appeals to both the ruthless commander who cares only about achieving his objective and nothing for the lives of his men, and to those heroic generals who wish to see the normal man, armed only with the humble lasgun, prevail against the hordes of bio-engineered aliens and Warp-spawned monstrosities that would otherwise tear the Imperium asunder. The Imperial Guard fights in vast formations and no other army in the 41st Millennium can field as many troops or powerful armoured battle tanks. The Imperial Guard pounds its foes to oblivion under a ceaseless torrent of lasgun volleys, battle-cannon fire and artillery bombardments.

HOW THIS CODEX WORKS

Codex: Imperial Guard contains the following sections:

- **The Imperial Guard:** The first section introduces the Imperial Guard, the Imperium's largest fighting force and their part in the Warhammer 40,000 universe. It includes full details of their history, their organisational structure, their raising and deployment to war zones across the entire galaxy. Also included are the backgrounds of many of the diverse regiments of the Imperial Guard and their actions during a millennia of bloody campaigns and brutal warfare on the battlefields of the 41st Millennium.

- **Forces of the Imperial Guard:** Each and every character, troop type and vehicle in the Imperial Guard army is examined in this section. Firstly, you will find a full description of the unit, describing its role within the army and its specialised combat abilities. Secondly, you will find complete rules for the unit and details of any unique skills, wargear or abilities they can use to crush the enemies of the Imperium.

- **Wargear:** This section contains full details and rules for the mass-produced and dependable weapons, armour and equipment used by the ranks of soldiers and armoured vehicles of the Imperial Guard.

- **Soldiers of the Imperial Guard:** This section contains colour photographs of the extensive range of Citadel miniatures available for your Imperial Guard army, gloriously painted by Games Workshop's famous 'Eavy Metal team. Colour schemes for various regiments are included.

- **Imperial Guard Army List:** The army list takes all of the units presented in the Forces of the Imperial Guard section and arranges them so you can choose an army for your own games. Each unit type also has a points value attached to help you pit your forces against an opponent's in a fair match.

FIND OUT MORE

While Codex: Imperial Guard contains everything you need to play a game with your army of Imperial Guardsmen, there are always more tactics to use, scenarios to fight and painting ideas to try out. The monthly magazine White Dwarf contains articles about all aspects of the Warhammer 40,000 game and hobby, and you can find articles specific to the Imperial Guard on our website:

www.games-workshop.com

THE IMPERIAL GUARD

The Imperial Guard comprises countless billions of soldiers drawn from a million worlds who stand against the innumerable threats that would see the Imperium of Man torn asunder. Serried ranks of soldiers and columns of steel-clad tanks face monstrous savages and inhuman horrors. The Imperial Guard forms the very backbone of the Imperium, without which Mankind would surely fall to the predations of aliens, heretics and worse.

The dominion of Man stretches from the Halo Stars to the Eastern Fringe and beyond. This gulf is unfathomably vast and travel from one end to the other is inconceivable during a mortal lifespan. Even communication between planets is an onerous and often unattainable task. Isolated by cosmic distances, a message sent at the speed of light would take many decades or even centuries to reach neighbouring star systems, cries for reinforcements going unheeded for aeons. Across this expansive realm there is only a single force numerous enough to defend all fronts simultaneously – the Imperial Guard – the Hammer of the Emperor.

As with all soldiers of the Imperium, the life of an Imperial Guardsman is one of discipline, duty and honour. Whilst such warriors are hardly the equal of Space Marines, they outnumber their superhuman brothers in arms by millions to one. Whilst the mass-reactive shell of a bolter can stop a single foe in its tracks, the hail of a million lasgun shots can halt the advance of an entire army. The forces of the Imperial Guard are trained to hold firm in the face of the enemy and respond with a steady aim. They fight neither with the most powerful weaponry nor with gene-enhanced metabolisms, but with fire in their bellies and courage in their hearts. That normal men do this in the face of bloodthirsty Daemons and towering alien bio-constructs makes it all the more heroic. Each Guardsman is sworn to protect the Emperor's realm and to annihilate his enemies in any of the terrible wars across the galaxy. It is warfare at its most brutal, where the lives of individual soldiers are irrelevant and the sacrifice of hundreds of thousands of men decides the fate of worlds. Yet even amongst such bloodbaths there are pivotal moments when the deeds of a company of brave troops can turn the tide. At such times the actions of even a single soldier can make the difference between victory and defeat.

The forces of the Imperial Guard are not subtle, responding to almost every situation with the application of overwhelming force. The Imperial Guard grinds its foes to nothing in gruelling wars of attrition, many commanders expending the lives of their men for the most trivial of tactical and strategic gains. Whilst certain resources, such as the relics from a lost technological age, are rare and priceless, the Imperium has at its disposal one currency so vast it is all but inexhaustible – manpower.

The logistics involved in transporting the colossal armies of the Imperial Guard are daunting; indeed, even getting the sprawling bulk of the Imperial Guard to a war zone is a victory in itself. Whilst the forces are unwieldy and slow to react, when such immense armies are deployed to engage the enemy the end result is inevitable. With such vast reservoirs of manpower, tanks and munitions, they are akin to a mighty sledgehammer that smashes its foes apart.

On the battlefield waves of infantry overwhelm enemy positions; those foes that are not killed by volleys of disciplined lasgun fire are likely to meet their fate on the end of a bayonet point or else trampled under the thundering charge of tens of thousands of boots. Lumbering beside these troops are mighty armoured battle tanks, rugged brutes of plas-steel and ceramite that bristle with firepower. These ponderous metal giants belch a fusillade of death and grind the enemy beneath heavy steel treads. The inexorable advance of the Imperial Guard is accompanied by the deafening roar of massive guns – enormous artillery barrages that pound the enemy into oblivion with shells that can topple a hab-block. By the strength of such armies have incalculable rebellions been crushed, relentless invading forces been shattered and entire alien empires been swept aside. It is through the sacrifice of the Imperial Guard that the Imperium of Man has endured for 10,000 years.

> "All of the million worlds of the Imperium shall look to their own defence. They shall also look to the defence of the Imperium, and to the prosecution of such wars as the Emperor in his wisdom shall decree, according to such requirements as shall be imposed by the Administratum. To this end each populated planet shall raise and maintain forces for its defence and, from its ranks, shall it provide the best of its troops for recruitment into the largest of the Imperium's armies – the Imperial Guard.
>
> Each Imperial Commander shall swear that such men as are given over to the defence of realms other than his own shall bear arms and be equipped to fight as befits an Imperial soldier, and that his domain shall stand ready with such mighty engines of war and machineries as are needed by his armies to crush the Imperium's enemies. The Imperial Commander shall understand that in this matter it is he, and he alone, who holds the responsibility for this undertaking. If his armies shall be found lacking or wanting in any regard, he shall no longer be fit for Lordship and shall face such censures or punishments as judged appropriate by the High Lord of Terra or their duly appointed agents."
>
> Introit to the Codex Exercitus,
> incorporating the Amalathian Oath.

THE HAMMER OF THE EMPEROR

The origins of the Imperial Guard date back to the Great Crusade when the Emperor conquered the stars and forged the Imperium of Man. At the forefront of this time of expansion and reclamation were the Space Marine Legions – the Adeptus Astartes – the finest warriors humanity had ever created, each the equal of a dozen normal men. Despite their formidable battle prowess, the forces of the Space Marines were not limitless, and the relentless demands of building a galactic empire pushed the Legions further apart. Separated by countless thousands of light years, their presence became ever more scattered and dilute. The Emperor required more manpower to ensure the momentum of the Great Crusade did not falter, and so the Imperial Army was created.

The Imperial Army was a vital part of the expedition fleets sent out to claim the stars in the Emperor's name. Gargantuan numbers of brave troops – millions growing to billions of men, ranks of armoured battle tanks and mighty armadas of spaceships were raised, all subordinate to the Legions Astartes. At first the Imperial Army was employed for garrison duties and mopping up resistance in the wake of the Legions, utilised where the back of an enemy was broken and compliance to the Imperium required only a watchful presence. Eventually, certainly by the time the Crusade reached the Eastern Fringe, the Imperial Army was deployed at the forefront of the Crusade, fighting alongside the power-armoured super-soldiers of the Adeptus Astartes.

This organisational structure all changed when the galaxy was ripped asunder by the treachery of the Warmaster Horus, triggering a cataclysmic civil war that engulfed the newly founded Imperium.

In the aftermath of the Horus Heresy, massive changes were implemented to the forces of the Imperium. To prevent the possibility of large-scale rebellion occurring again, the titanic armies of the Imperial forces were divided. The Space Marine Legions were split into Chapters. The Imperial Army, as it was, ceased to exist. The link between fleet and army was severed – never again would ground commanders be given direct control over interstellar ships. From its ashes were born the Imperial Navy and the Imperial Guard. The Imperial Guard was reorganised into smaller units known as regiments, and centrally trained Commissars were universally introduced to watch out for disloyalty. The inter-dependence of the newly formed Imperial Guard, the most numerous of the Emperor's troops, ensured that should a regiment turn against their oaths they would not be able to spread their treachery beyond a single world, and should a Navy fleet mutiny then they would not have the ability to re-supply or deploy ground troops. The Imperium had learnt a painful lesson following the dark days of the Horus Heresy.

"Peace? There cannot be peace in these times"

Lord Solar Macharius

Strategic Command

In theory, Imperial Guard Officers receive their orders from the Lord Commander of their respective Segmentum Commands, who are in turn enacting the wishes of the High Lords of Terra. In practice, the immense distances and delays in communication between worlds often makes a mockery of such procedures and the sheer scale of the Imperium prevents any meaningful central control. Operational control of any given army group is therefore assigned to a high-ranking Imperial Officer such as a general, high marshal or even lord hetman who assumes responsibility for completion of his given duties. This might be the initiation of a decade-long conflict to cleanse a star-system of savage greenskins, or it could involve the protection of adamantium mines or promethium refineries from pirate raids. Just as common are the military recolonisations of planets lost from the Imperium's fold. Whatever his task, the commander of such an army group has the responsibility for the deployment and application of all resources at his disposal; innumerable waves of infantry companies, ranks of battle tanks, batteries of artillery weapons, and a host of other specialist troops and tools of war. Some commanders yearn to lead such forces on the battlefield, hungry for glory and honour. They establish a front line headquarters and personally lead their men in battle, banners and pennants proclaiming the officer's many deeds and victories so that his troops are emboldened and enemies might tremble at his sheer presence. Others consider their abilities far too important and valuable to be exposed to front line conflicts. Surrounded by a host of advisors, data-globes, and parchment bearing servo-skulls, they direct their forces from the relative safety of an orbiting starship, a Proteus-class battle bunker or the lumbering armoured bulk of a Leviathan command vehicle.

There are very rare circumstances in which a higher level of command is necessary. In these times the rank of Warmaster is bestowed upon a mighty and brilliant leader. This rank is not available to the Departmento Munitorum without the express consent of the High Lords of Terra, and such an individual is said to wield authority second only to the Emperor himself. Several centuries can pass without a Warmaster being appointed and because of the unrivalled power of the position there is never more than one in existence at any one time. Due to the stigma associated with the title and the Arch-traitor Horus, it is not uncommon for other titles to used in place of Warmaster, the most famous being Lord Solar.

The Departmento Munitorum

The Departmento Munitorum is the military arm of the Administratum and forms the general staff of the Imperial Guard. It is a mammoth bureaucratic organisation responsible for the distribution of every aspect of the Imperial Guard's military resources. Perhaps its most important function concerns the monitoring of tithes and the raising and transportation of the Imperial Guard between war zones – for which it liaises with the Imperial Navy. Without the adepts and scribes of the Departmento Munitorum the vast armies of the Imperial Guard would stagnate and calls for aid would go unanswered. The mighty war-fleets of the Imperial Navy would not intercept enemy invasions, the armies of Mankind would never push back the relentless attacks. Slowly but surely the isolated worlds would fall, and the Imperium would ultimately be lost.

A plea for military aid may come to the ears of the Imperium, but not be acted upon for months, years or even decades. Such requests typically make their way through countless adepts before finally reaching the hands of one who can sanction suitable action, sitting at a dimly lit pulpit-station many hundreds of light years away. One such example occurred when a battle group consisting of over a dozen regiments from Mordant and Tremert were raised to eliminate unknown xenos forces on the planet of Hurspraxia, only to arrive over a century too late, finding a lifeless world with no trace of survivors.

Organised at the sector and subsector level, every echelon of the Departmento Munitorum has enough autonomy to respond to problems within local star-systems. With the vagaries of Warp travel and communication, this is essential. Their smaller size allows the individual subsectors can respond to emergent threats more quickly and as such, when one comes under attack, an army group is formed from the regiments of all worlds in the local star systems.

When raising an army group the Departmento Munitorum is responsible for munitions, supplies, recruitment, training, medical and technical support. The methods by which forces accumulate are haphazard at best, many thousands of troops from dozens of regiments across several worlds are raised and directed to the appropriate war zone. The unpredictable nature of the Warp and the inherent dangers of interstellar travel are such that it is not unusual for entire regiments to be lost or even destroyed in transit. Some may be delayed by the ravages of Warpstorms or appear from the Immaterium many thousands of light years from their destination. That sufficient troops arrive at a crisis point is only because of the sheer mass of troops and vehicles despatched by the Departmento Munitorum in the first place.

> "I have at my command an entire battle group of the Imperial Guard. Fifty regiments, including specialised drop troops, stealthers, mechanised formations, armoured companies and mobile artillery. Over half a million fighting men and thirty thousand tanks and artillery pieces are mine to command.
>
> Emperor show mercy to the fool who stands against me, for I shall not."
>
> Warmaster Demetrius, Salonika Crusade, 733.M38

Recruitment

Every Imperial Commander in the Imperium, also known as a Planetary Lord or Imperial Governor, is responsible for the defence of their world. This is crucial as a planet may need to defend itself against the predations of a myriad of nefarious enemies for many months, or even years, before reinforcements arrive. To this end, they are duty bound to recruit, equip, train and maintain a fighting force. On some planets this may take the form of an official military or a garrison force. On other worlds the duty to defend their world may fall to dozens of seperate armies, tribes and hive gangs, some of which may even be warring factions who unite to oppose an invading foe. In any case, these forces are unlikely to ever leave the confines of their home world.

As part of their annual tithe Imperial Governors are obliged to send no less than one tenth of their overall fighting force, and as much more as the Departmento Munitorum deem necessary, to fight the Emperor's wars throughout the galaxy. This is the most important aspect of the tribute for it is these regiments that form the Imperial Guard. The exact number of regiments that are to be raised for the Imperial Guard will depend upon the individual world's tithe grade and its proximity to hostile warzones. For a hive world such as Armageddon, caught in the throes of an all-consuming war, a draft of at least a hundred million men at arms and several million armoured vehicles is typical – a tiny fraction of the total populace which numbers in the hundreds of billions. A far-flung agri-world may have a significantly lower military tribute, perhaps as few as five million men and cavalry, but

this may be a significant proportion of the world's population. In any case, should a tithe be of an unacceptable quality, the Imperial Governor's life is forfeit. For this reason those soldiers selected for the Imperial Guard tend to be drawn from the elite of a planet's troops.

Methods of recruiting vary from world to world. On the Chaos-plagued world of Cadia every man, woman and child is expected to serve in the Cadian Defence Force and, by extension, the Imperial Guard. On seething hive worlds such as Alcatran, it is common for entire generations to be drafted and sent to fight on distant worlds, the indentured gangs given the choice between volunteering or summary execution. On many planets service in the Imperial Guard is seen as noble and brings much honour to the ruling houses. Many young hopefuls, especially on industrial worlds and factory planets, flock to the world's military forces in the hope of being found worthy of the Imperial Guard – often the only chance of escape from their claustrophobic existence and endless work shifts. It is not unusual for the elite units of a planet to compete for promotion to the Imperial Guard. On some of the more savage frontier worlds, these competitions can escalate into affairs that claim as many lives as a small war.

Upon their initial founding, regiments are identified by the name of their home world and a number – for example, the 144th Cadian Regiment is the one hundred and forty fourth regiment to have been raised on the fortress world of Cadia. It is not uncommon for a regiment's number to be recycled following its destruction, a new raising taking the designation of their predecessor. In this way the regiment is re-founded, the new recruits tasked with upholding its honour and traditions. Indeed, the Vintor 823rd serve the Emperor to this day, despite being wiped out on more than nine different occasions in the span of a single decade. In addition, regiments are often given unofficial names, either inherited and therefore part of tradition, or else earned on the field of battle. For example, the Catachan VII 'Catachan Devils' Regiment take the name of the apex predator from the lethal confines of their fetid death world, whereas the Cadian 8th Regiment, 'The Lord Castellan's Own', honour the exploits of their former commanding officer, Lord Castellan Ursarkar Creed.

> "What I cannot crush with words I will crush with the tanks of the Imperial Guard!"
>
> Lord Solar Macharius

The uniforms and specific armaments of the different Imperial Guard regiments changes dramatically from world to world. Upon their raising, each regiment is equipped in the manner of their home world. The newly inducted Imperial Guardsmen are issued with the same style of uniform and weapons as that of their own world's fighting forces. The troopers may go to war in full battle-dress or little more than primitive armour and tribal tattoos. The only universal piece of equipment common throughout the entirety of the Imperial Guard is the lasgun. This weapon is cheap and easy to manufacture, extremely reliable and simple to maintain. The lasgun is therefore ideally suited to arm the massed armies of the Imperial Guard.

Regimental Organisation

Each regiment is raised from a single planet, and because of this troopers of the Imperial Guard regard themselves as belonging first and foremost to their regiment rather than the army or battle group to which they are assigned.

On their home worlds, the forces who serve to defend the planet may have been split into battalions, divisions, cohorts, militia groups, geno-corps and a host of other formations, but, in the Imperial Guard there is only the regiment. The concept of what exactly comprises a regiment is not at first glance an easily quantifiable matter, the huge variations in troop and vehicle dispositions making no two seem alike.

An Imperial Guard regiment is largely uniform in its composition. Infantry regiments, for example, are unlikely to contain much or any heavy artillery, whilst tank regiments contain little or no infantry. Success requires Imperial Guard regiments to work together. Whilst this interdependence may at first seem like an inherent weakness, it is a necessary precaution. Should a regiment rebel against the Emperor, the traitors will not have access to the supporting units needed to prosecute a full-scale war. When the Ocanan XV Infantry declared its allegiance to the Ruinous Powers of Chaos it had little in the way of either heavy armour or artillery support and was unable to compete against the 'combined arms' forces of the Cadian 17th Armoured and Elysian 110th Drop-troop regiments sent to eliminate them.

Regiments are typically raised with a strength of several thousand soldiers but the precise numbers can vary enormously. The Valhallan 18th Light Infantry 'Tundra Wolves' consists of over one hundred and twenty thousand men whilst the Vostroyan Heavy Armoured 24th 'Iron Bloods' comprised less than one and a half thousand tank crewmen. Regiments of Baneblades and Shadowswords, each an armoured behemoth capable of laying waste to a small army by itself, rarely consist of more than a dozen super-heavy tanks. The basic principle held by the Departmento Munitorum is that regardless of number of men at arms or the exact composition of armoured vehicles, the overall fighting strength – and hence combat effectiveness – of one regiment is equivalent to any other. This is clearly a gross oversimplification but a necessary one when organising wars on a galactic scale.

Imperial Guard regiments are divided into several companies according to a complex set of templates detailed in the Tactica Imperialis, each placed under the command of a senior officer. The number of companies in a regiment depends upon the type and size of the forces at the commander's disposal, but may consist of as few as three or as many as twenty. Companies are themselves organised into several platoons, typically between three and six. Platoons are typically comprised of a Platoon Command Squad and several ten-man Infantry Squads – the most numerous of the Imperial Guard's forces.

Support units, such as heavy weapons platoons and much valued specialist units, such as battle tanks, artillery, and abhuman squads, may be attached to a company for a single battle or entire duration of a campaign. These are rarely permanent additions and are attached as needed by the regimental commanders. It is a common practice, especially

amongst armoured and artillery regiments, to break down several companies and second them to infantry forces, in exchange for platoons to provide close support from the attentions of enemy troops. If serving together for extended durations attached units tend to adopt their foster-regiment's uniform and unit markings. This not only has the practicality of helping to avoid friendly-fire incidents, but it aids in promoting comradeship with the soldiers they will be fighting and dying alongside.

Deployment and Training

Should an Imperial planet come under attack and the local defences prove insufficient, an Imperial Commander is entitled to request aid from the Departmento Munitorum, for which its primary response will be the deployment of the Imperial Guard. As war descends upon neighbouring systems new regiments will be raised and army groups formed, drawn from the resources of all nearby planets. When an army is assembled regiments are drawn from many different planets, resulting in a conglomeration of uniforms and combat skills rather than a single homogenous force. Bio-screened techno-troopers fight side by side with primitive barbarians and noble-born soldiers rub shoulders with the lowliest gang fighters. When Waaagh! Grax invaded the Ryza system in 925.M41, all planets within ten light years were ordered to recruit and raise at least an additional fifty regiments as a primary reaction to counter the Ork invasion. Should the Imperium's response not prove to be decisive in crushing an enemy then the sphere around the conflict zone is increased in ever-larger increments, reinforcements will be drawn from further away and more regiments are raised to replace the losses. This ponderous process repeats itself until the enemy is ground down and destroyed, the massed forces of the Imperial Guard slowly pounding at the foe until eventually the hammer blow is delivered and all resistance is completely and utterly shattered. In this way, the harder a foe strikes at the Imperium, the greater its response will be.

Many of the newly raised regiments inducted into the Imperial Guard will already have some modicum of fighting experience. This may have taken the form of formal military instruction or simply be the result of the instincts necessary to stay alive on their respective home worlds. Only the strongest survive the gang wars inherent on hive worlds, the tribal conflicts on a medieval feudal world or the carnivorous predators that stalk a death world. In any case, during the long voyage between their home world and the regiment's destination, the newly inducted Guardsmen will receive intensive training that tempers the natural fighting skills of their many disparate cultures and forges them into soldiers worthy of the Imperial Guard. They are trained in the use of specialised weaponry and vehicles and receive proper indoctrination into the Imperial Cult. Officers are tutored in the broader aspects of the Tactica Imperialis, all the while being judged under the vigilant gaze of the Commissariat. The regiment will be drilled for many weeks before their trial by fire in the crucible of war. The training is also intended to adapt and, where necessary, re-educate the new recruits for the inevitable shock of fighting on foreign worlds. It is unlikely that a Guardsman from the monolithic spires of a hive city has ever seen the open sky, whilst those from a backwater agri-world will never have seen the towering might of a mountain-sized basilica sanctum or set foot inside the twisting labyrinth of a sprawling factorum-city.

Should a regiment survive a campaign it is unlikely it will return to its home world, moving instead from one warzone to another. As casualties reduce the overall strength of fighting forces, regiments are often amalgamated together so that united, they can continue to wage the Emperor's wars. Where possible, two half-strength regiments from the same home world will combine, but it is not uncommon for two disparate cultures to find themselves brothers in arms. Many commanders declare that the reduced efficiency of these combined regiments makes them barely worth their rations; infighting and mistrust hampering their battlefield effectiveness. Other commanders are interested only in the number of men-at-arms that can be fielded, their successful integration as fighting units a secondary concern.

If a regiment has been so badly mauled that it is considered a waste of time and resources to combine it with other Imperial forces, they may be assigned garrison duties over a nearby world, usually the very same planet they have been fighting over. The safety of the world and its population becomes the duty of the regiment's remnants. The garrisoning of such

worlds is vital. After a brutal war in which the local defence forces are inevitably decimated and the government left in tatters, the small Imperial Guard contingent may be the only loyal force left to impose law and maintain control for many decades. In rare circumstances, a regiment may be granted custodianship over a world as a reward. The officers of such forces inevitably become wealthy and powerful figures in the society they maintain watch over, forming the new noble and ruling classes.

The Schola Progenium

The Schola Progenium nurtures the orphan sons and daughters of Imperial officials from all over the galaxy. They are tutored to love the Emperor and to desire nothing more than to serve him and the Imperium to the best of their abilities. They tolerate no disloyalty and remain ever vigilant for signs of treachery. Many who pass through the hands of the Schola Progenium are initiated into the Adeptus Terra. Some find their way into the Inquisition, and the most studious and zealous are welcomed by the Ecclesiarchy.

For natural warriors the Imperial Guard offers a place in one of the elite Storm Trooper companies, where the training received is of a brutally high standard. A few individuals, those who are both natural leaders and are fiercely loyal, attract the attentions of the Commissariat. Commissars provide the link between regimental officers and the Departmento Munitorum. They are tough, ruthless individuals whose primary responsibilities are to preserve the courage, discipline and loyalty of the regiment. Commissars have the absolute authority to punish and execute any member of a regiment who fails in their duties. As Commissars are not from the same world as the regiment they serve with, they are not coloured by that world's traditions and culture. Instead a Commissar can provide an objective and unbiased viewpoint, one seen purely from the Imperium's perspective.

> "Weep for him, for his faith was not sufficient. Rejoice for yourselves, for my faith is bottomless! Forward, for the Emperor!"
>
> Commissar Krieglust

The Adeptus Ministorum

The Adeptus Ministorum, also known as the Ecclesiarchy, is responsible for maintaining the faith of the masses of Mankind and adherence to any of its various cults and multitudinous creeds. The different methods of worshipping the Emperor are as numerous as the stars themselves. Some Priests of the Adeptus Ministorum found their faith in scriptures and dogma or mighty edifices raised in the Emperor's name. Others are but simple men who have devoted their life to tending to the Emperor's flock and illuminating the ignorant to his majestic glory. Nowhere are the God-Emperor's benedictions and fervour needed more than on the battlefield, and devoted preachers are a common sight in the Imperial Guard. The Ecclesiarch has decreed that every regiment should be accompanied by at least one adept from the Ministorum but it is not uncommon for more to flock to martyr themselves on the battlefield. Indeed, the regiments raised from amongst the pious people of Athanos regularly have several Priests per company.

The Machine Cult of Mars

Known by many as the Priesthood of Mars, it is the Adeptus Mechanicus who have knowledge of the arcane lores and mysteries that maintain the ancient technologies of the Imperium. It is their duty to tend to the machine spirits of the Imperium's vehicles and observe correct reverence to the Machine God.

The vehicles and wargear used by the Imperial Guard are rugged, durable and, most importantly of all, simple to manufacture. Industrial worlds churn out thousands of Leman Russ Battle Tanks and Chimera Armoured Transports every day. Large, grinding production lines manned by thousands of work gangs toil ceaselessly in the manufactorums to meet their quotas. A small number of planets, known as forge worlds, are capable of maintaining the more advanced weapons of the Imperium – relics from the Dark Age of Technology. Knowledge of their creation is a long forgotten art, the science behind their construction debased to myth and superstitious rites. These ancient technologies are jealously guarded and even revered by the Adeptus Mechanicus, these potent weapons of war can turn the tide of a battle.

Before being transported to a warzone a newly raised Imperial Guard regiment may receive additional units from a forge world. Adepts of the Machine Cult of Mars – the Techpriest Enginseers – also attach themselves to regiments at this time in order to provide the Imperial Guard with advanced technical support.

Super-heavy Tanks

The largest of Imperial Guard armies may be supported by the mighty warmachines of the super-heavy tank regiments. Though each regiment may contain only a dozen or fewer vehicles, and they rarely fight side by side, each super-heavy is the equal of an entire company of other troops in terms of sheer offensive power. The most common of these vehicles is the Baneblade, which bristles with every type of weapon from heavy flamer to massive-bore cannon. Other, specialised types include the Titan-hunting Shadowsword and the infantry-killing Stormlord. The mere sight of a super-heavy tank has been known to rout entire armies.

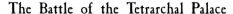

Abhuman Regiments

Abhumans are human-descended creatures such as Ratlings or Ogryns, whose physical appearance and mental capabilities are quite different from that of their ancestors. Many abhuman settlements were purged during the Age of Apostasy and even today they are regarded with mistrust by many of their human comrades. Despite this, abhumans have proved loyal to the Imperium, adapting their skills and attributes to the Emperor's wars. Abhuman home worlds are few and far between, and the total populations are not particularly high. This results in relatively few abhuman regiments being raised each year for the Imperial Guard. Because abhumans have very specific areas of competence it is usual to divide these regiments into smaller units that are attached to other formations for the duration of a particular campaign. In this way the expertise granted by abhumans is not limited to a single regiment alone.

The Scholastica Psykana

The Scholastica Psykana is the psychic training organisation of the Adeptus Astra Telepathica. Their primary responsibility is the safeguarding of Mankind from human psykers who would use their powers for nefarious means. As such, all psykers must be tested and they are transported from their home worlds in one of the infamous Black Ships. Under the steely gaze of the Inquisition the dangerous, weak, possessed and insane are weeded out. From the rest will be prepared the many psychic servants required by the Adeptus Terra. Most will travel to Holy Terra, there to be consumed as they become part of the psychic choir of the Astronomican, the beacon that shines in the Warp and allows the Navigators to travel through the Immaterium. Other, more powerful psykers will undergo the Soul Binding ritual and become one of the mysterious Astropaths whose psychic communications hold the Imperium together. These tormented souls are vital as they afford the only viable means of communicating over interstellar distances, transmitting thoughts and dreams to others of their kind. As with everything associated with the Warp, however, astrotelepathy is an erratic process. The psychic messages transmitted by Astropaths are affected by the currents, eddies and storms of the Immaterium. The consequence of this unpredictability means that it may take mere moments, several days or many decades for an Astropath's signal to reach its destination. Tales abound of messages arriving before even being sent, astropathic echoes of the future that reverberate through the unreality of Warp-space, the understanding of which defies mortal comprehension.

More potent, but less numerous still, are the individuals that have been judged suitable for battle-training. Carefully monitored, these Sanctioned Psykers are trained to use their otherworldly abilities to smite the Emperor's enemies in the fires of war.

The use of psykers in the Imperial Guard is regarded by the superstitious as a necessary evil – one that is tolerated with a mixture of awe, fear and, most of all, suspicion.

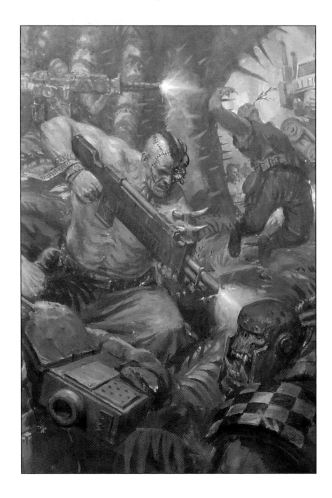

The Battle of the Tetrarchal Palace

The greatest battle to have been fought upon the world of Mordian is one which few records describe in anything but the most vague of terms. The battle was against the hordes of Chaos, and the Inquisition have purged all archives lest the taint of the Warp infect those who read of them. In this battle, Mordian was almost entirely drowned beneath a tidal wave of daemonic filth brought into being by cultists and traitors within the population. At the last, the Mordian Iron Guard held only one final strongpoint, the Tetrarchal Palace, but they never surrendered in the face of the abominations of Chaos. It is said that not a single Mordian took a step back when surrounded by the daemonic hordes, each man determined to fight to the death.

It was as the daemonic hordes launched their final charge that the sky was suddenly filled with the glittering lights of spacecraft – relief had come. Whilst the Mordians had stood, fought, and died holding back the innumerable hordes of Chaos, the Imperium had gathered a mighty convocation of the most potent of psykers. Together, the psykers had wrought a counter-spell the like of which had not been seen since the Horus Heresy. The psykers' gestalt will had fought a duel with the very Gods of Chaos, and, for a time at least, they succeeded in repelling the Daemons and saving Mordian. Whilst the cost in lives was high the courage, discipline and sacrifice of the Iron Guard spared Mordian from a fate too terrible to comprehend.

LORD SOLAR MACHARIUS

Lord Solar Macharius was one of the greatest war leaders the Imperium has ever known; a military genius without compare whose dreams of conquest reshaped the Imperium.

At the dawn of the 41st Millennium, Lord Solar Macharius, most successful and brilliant of Warmasters since Horus, finished leading an uncompromising seven-year crusade that swept through the Segmentum Pacificus and brought no less than a thousand worlds back into the Imperial fold. The Lord Solar's great armies fought at the very border of intergalactic space and even reached into the Halo Zone, just beyond the edge of the Segmentum Pacificus, where not even the blessed light of the Astronomican can permeate through the dark void.

Many men have been dubbed insane for putting into practice what Saints have preached. Lord Solar Machaius was such a man. However, whilst some called him a monster and a madman, others saw a determined visionary. In life Macharius was a brutal conqueror and a ruthless soldier. He was a brilliant and callous strategist. No one has led the armies of the Imperial Guard to more victories or to greater conquests, nor won so many worlds for the Imperium since the Great Crusade.

The Lord Solar's forces consisted of seven whole army groups, each led by a general appointed by the Warmaster himself. Macharius was able to coordinate strategy on any scale, from a contained battlefield where tactics were organised at the squad and platoon level, to system-wide campaigns involving dozens of regiments fighting over several planets. Macharius was a ruthless commander who ordered the bombardment of planets until they submitted and commanded the extermination of entire worlds. Nothing would stop Macharius nor stall the momentum of his armies' advance. Those worlds that could not be conquered were mercilessly destroyed. The Lord Solar's fiery oratory was legendary and whenever he personally commanded his soldiers they shared in his passion and would throw themselves into the most horrendous battle with vigour and determination. The Lord Solar was never far from the front lines, where he could see and feel the flow of battle and inspire his men to victory. His presence on the battlefield was said to be worth that of fifty thousand men and legends insist that many enemies surrendered at the mere mention of his name. Macharius' personal victories are documented in the histories of the Imperium, drawn from the accounts of the Warmaster's very own generals. It is written that Macharius led the blitz on the fortified world of Kallastin, conquering the entire planet in only a single day. The histories of this magnificent achievement state that at the battle's zenith Macharius split apart the great Iron Wall with but a single word, a voice that not even the mighty battlements could oppose.

Though Macharius was prepared to capture a thousand more worlds, his armies could not. The Lord Solar's armies had been pushed to exhaustion by the relentless pace with which Macharius had driven them. Furthermore, many of his troops whispered that the stars of the Halo Zone were haunted and the worlds which orbited them were inhabited by ghosts. It is said that Macharius wept hot tears of rage and disappointment as he gazed upon the distant stars that would forever remain beyond his grasp, defeated not by any opposing warlords, but by human fear and frailty. Reluctantly, Macharius agreed to conclude his campaign and return to the Imperium. The Lord Solar was never seen alive again, for he died during the voyage back to his home world. The exact nature of Macharius' death remains shrouded in mystery.

> "The meaning of victory is not to merely defeat your enemy but to destroy him, to completely eradicate him from living memory, to leave no remnant of his endeavours, to crush utterly his achievement and remove from all record his every trace of existence. From that defeat no enemy can ever recover. That is the meaning of victory."
>
> Lord Solar Macharius

In death Lord Solar Macharius is revered as a Saint. He is immortalised as one of the Imperium's greatest heroes and his body is interred in a great sepulchre on his home world, renamed Macharia in his honour. It is said that at the Lord Solar's funeral march over a million men filed past his tomb and a hundred privileged officers laid their swords upon his marbled sarcophagus. Foremost amongst these swords are the six blades that the Lord Solar gifted to his army group generals at the outset of the Macharian Conquests. The decommissioned Emperor-class battleship *Lord of Light*, the Lord Solar's second flagship during his legendary campaign, now orbits the shrine world of Macharia as a tribute to his many victories.

After his death, Macharius' old generals could not hold his conquests together. Their own rivalry erupted into civil war and the conquered territories divided into warring military empires led by Imperial Commanders who abandoned their oaths of loyalty to the Imperium. The Macharian Heresy, as this period of struggle is called, was finally ended by a crusade in which almost one hundred Space Marine Chapters took part. The majority of the worlds conquered by Macharius were successfully re-pacified and now form a substantial and prosperous part of the Imperium. The heresy lasted for almost seventy years; a testament to the astonishing speed and wide extent of the Lord Solar's original conquests.

Even though a millennia has passed, Macharius' name, deeds, vision and teachings are still honoured throughout the Imperium.

FAMOUS REGIMENTS OF THE IMPERIAL GUARD

There are a million worlds in the Imperium and the regiments raised on each have their own culture, language, equipment and fighting styles. In battle these differences are quickly eroded and bonds of comradeship are soon forged as the disparate troopers fight and die together, united against a common foe.

CADIAN SHOCK TROOPS

The entire population of Cadia is destined for a military life, the birth rate and recruitment rate being synonymous. The Cadian Shock Troop regiments are highly disciplined and have a reputation for being excellent shots. Indeed, a child of Cadia is taught how to strip, reassemble and shoot a lasgun before they can read or write. Cadian regiments march to war in uniform patterns, camouflaged in a manner most suited to the mixed terrain of the Cadian wilderness. As Cadians manufacture excellent military equipment their regiments are equipped with only the finest weapons.

Cadia has a special and honoured place in the history of Mankind. It stands upon the edge of the Eye of Terror within a narrow corridor of stable space called the Cadian Gate, the only stable passage between the Chaos infested Daemon worlds of the Eye of Terror and the Imperium. No battlefleet of any size can rely upon other passages, but must pass through the Cadian Gate. Cadia is therefore one of the most strategically important planets in the galaxy.

On numerous occasions the forces of the Ruinous Powers have moved against Cadia and raging battles have been fought in the depths of space. However, the merciless forces of Chaos do not limit their intrusions to space lanes. Raids and landings upon populated worlds in the Cadian system are commonplace. As such, all Cadians must train in the defence forces, and many are drafted into the Imperial Guard. Before induction, all Cadians must first serve in the Youth Army, joining one of the so-called Whiteshield platoons who are distinguished by a white stripe running from the front to back of their helmets. It is considered a rite of passage on Cadia to serve in one of the Whiteshield platoons and the troopers are eager to show their worth and prove themselves in the crucible of war.

> *"Any Cadian who can't field-strip his own lasgun by age ten was born on the wrong planet"*
>
> Anon

Cadian officers are well versed in the doctrines of the Tactica Imperium and are highly lauded for their implementation of both strategy and tactics. These officers exemplify the Cadian code of discipline and self-sacrifice that all Cadians aspire to. The Cadian Shock Troop regiments tend to have a high proportion of Veteran Squads. Formed from the survivors of the harshest warzones, these proven warriors may receive additional training and special armaments. Only the toughest survive the punishing training regimes, but to serve in the Cadian elite is considered a great honour. Each soldier is expected to act above and beyond the call of duty – they are some of the finest troops in the Imperial Guard.

The Cadian 8th 'The Lord Castellan's Own'

The Cadian 8th Infantry Regiment proudly bears the title of 'The Lord Castellan's Own', for the regiment is able to boast none other than the Lord Castellan of Cadia, Ursarkar E. Creed, as a former Colonel. Despite the fact that Creed has long since ascended to the general staff, he remains the Colonel-in-Chief of the 8th, and has led them in battle on many occasions since. The Cadian 8th enjoys a privileged position amongst the Shock Troopers, its companies providing an honour guard to the highest-ranking members of Cadia's military government. Its officers are in great demand amongst other Cadian regiments, and they often serve detached duty training newly raised units, ensuring the martial traditions and combat skills of the Cadian Shock Troop regiments are passed on from one generation to the next.

CATACHAN JUNGLE FIGHTERS

The men forming the Catachan regiments are tough, resourceful and uncompromising warriors. They excel at fast-moving, close-quarter fire-fights, infiltration and sniper work. Each Catachan is a born survivor, hardened to the very core. These courageous people have endured one of the most dangerous and perilous ordeals known to Mankind – growing up on the very planet of their birth.

Catachan is a death world, perhaps the most notorious and dangerous of all death worlds in the Imperium. Every native creature is a carnivore and every form of plant life is poisonous. Catachan is a planet so inimical to human life that every day there is a battle for survival. With a gruesome mortality rate, only the toughest survive to reach adulthood. Half the population dies before they can learn to walk, and half again perish before they reach ten years of age. There are no mineral or strategic assets on Catachan, its people have but one resource of value to the Imperium; their superb regiments of Jungle Fighters. Catachan warriors readily accept the call to arms and, in exchange for this tithe of warriors, their settlements receive supplies from the Imperium that would otherwise be impossible to obtain.

Common to all the soldiers of the Catachan regiments are red bandanas, symbolic of the blood-oath each warrior takes when he joins the regiment, and steel-alloy knives. A well-honed Catachan blade is not only a tool and a weapon amongst these fighters, but also a mark of their status.

Catachans take great pride that their officers, renowned hunters and esteemed warriors all, share with the troopers every danger and hardship. As such, discipline in the Catachan regiments is maintained through trust and respect as well as rank. The Jungle Fighter regiments tend to be fiercely independent as a result and outsiders, particularly authoritative figures such as Commissars, have difficulty in earning the Catachans' deference.

Catachans have a reputation for reckless bravery that borders on the insane. This is reflected in the dangers they willingly throw themselves into and their preferred choice of weaponry. Flamers and demolition charges, armaments that can be as deadly to the user as the enemy, are commonplace; the specialists who wield them are well known for their claims that such weapons wouldn't dare harm a Catachan. The Catachan regiments can also boast some of the best snipers in the Imperial Guard. Catachan marksmen will take up position hours, or even days, before a battle, in order to get the best vantage point.

> "We've run into scorpions the size of battle tanks. Three men died from Eyerot last week and I've sweated enough to fill a lake. Emperor help me, I love this place – it's just like home!"
>
> Captain Rock commenting on Varestus Prime.

Catachan tank crews typically adorn their vehicles with non-standard stylised decals, kill-markings and unofficial nicknames in addition to standard army badges. Sentinel pilots in particular personalise and modify their vehicles to better suit each individual warrior's particular combat style.

The warriors of Catachan do not think highly of medals, and see them as little more than baubles. Instead, achievements of merit are typically marked out by tattoos. Skull motifs are common amongst veterans that have served for more than five years. Dagger symbols are used by those that survive ten years. Ever practical, Catachans dull their regimental badges with soot and soil so as not to reflect light and give away the soldier's position to an enemy.

Catachan XVIII 'Swamp Rats'

The Catachan 'Swamp Rats', led by Colonel Gator, fought for seven years against a Tyranid infestation on the world of Koralkal VIII. During this time the Swamp Rats were forced to develop many unorthodox tactics to combat the Tyranid menace. Teams of highly experienced 'nid hunters covered their bodies in the ichor of the aliens they had slain, to build up an immunity to the aliens' toxins and also to mask their own scent from the Tyranid organisms that hunted them in turn. The Catachans were thus able to lie in ambush, using the pheromone glands cut from slaughtered Lictors to lure the bulk of the Tyranid swarms into carefully constructed, booby trapped, fire-zones. After successfully eliminating the Tyranids, the surviving soldiers of the Swamp Rats had to spend two years on board a decontamination ship.

MORDIAN IRON GUARD

Mordians are grim and dour by nature, respecting only discipline and duty. Their regiments are fiercely loyal to their cause: the prosecution of the Emperor's enemies. The Mordian Iron Guard are superbly drilled soldiers. In battle they present perfectly formed ranks of troops to the enemy, unleashing precisely timed volleys of las-fire from behind a hedge of bayonet points.

There is no concept of daybreak or nightfall on Mordian, for the planet rotates so slowly that the same side is forever pointing towards its sun. As a result, this side of Mordian is continuously bathed in radiation, leaving it a scorched and lifeless wasteland of splintered rock and canyons. On Mordian, all life exists on the opposite side of the planet, which lies in perpetual darkness. It is for this reason that Mordian is also known as the World of Eternal Night.

The side of Mordian that can support life seethes with people crammed into pyramidal, multi-levelled towers that rise like mountains. It is a crowded world where all resources are tightly controlled, and rationed. Crime and discontent are rife and the only thing that stands between order and total anarchy is the martial code of the Iron Guard.

The Mordian Iron Guard regiments march to war in bright colours and ornate uniforms. Some enemies of the Emperor have been misled by the sight of the Iron Guard, believing they were fighting amateurs, only to find tough, determined, professional soldiers. Upon each regiment's founding, a lavish banner, created within Mordian's Tetrarchal Palace, is presented to the regiment in a parade ground ceremony during which every Guardsman swears an oath to never let the colours fall in battle or be captured by the enemy.

The soldiers raised on Mordian have a reputation for following orders to the letter, and without a moment's hesitation. In battle, these troops will continue to reload and fire until either they, or the enemy, are annihilated. Each Guardsman rigidly obeys and respects the chain of command and the Iron Guard are amongst the most dependable troops in the Imperial Guard. Mordian tank crews are as disciplined as the infantry, their training as strict and rigorous as is humanly possible.

The vehicles and soldiers of Mordian Iron Guard regiments proudly display an Iron Eagle emblem in addition to regular platoon, company and army markings, reminding the Mordians to enforce the Emperor's steely discipline throughout the Imperium.

> "They may spend every off-duty minute polishing their shiny boots and marching up and down the parade ground in perfect formation, but don't let that fool you. These men are steel-eyed, cold-blooded killers and I'd as soon have a platoon of them in my force as I would a company of other troops."
>
> Gharan O'Hen, Army 212 Chief of Staff,
> on the Mordian Iron Guard.

The 3rd Mordian

The third regiment of the Mordian Iron Guard are the most decorated regiment in their home world's proud history of service to the Imperium. It was during the defence of Hive Barbarossa against Waaagh! Dregruk that the Mordian regiment faced a horde of barbaric Orks at the Battle of the Marble Garden.

Amongst statues of great heroes, around tinkling fountains and across imported Luptian bluegrass lawns, the Mordians made their stand. Despite rigid volleys of platoon fire gunning down hundreds of Orks, a column of light vehicles managed to outflank the Mordians and penetrate their lines. It was then that Colonel Grauer committed his reserves – a company of Hellhound Flame Tanks and a squadron of Leman Russ Exterminators. The tanks rumbled into the fray, the guns of the Exterminators blazing, each fusillade cutting a bloody swathe through the tightly packed hordes of savage greenskins. The Hellhounds crashed into the Ork ranks and dozens of greenskins were consumed in the conflagration. As their death-howls screamed over the crackling of flames, the Ork horde began to fall back from this fresh onslaught. The Mordian infantry then responded, advancing by platoon to pour more fire into the retreating Orks. Those few Orks that survived fled to the deepest reaches of the hive, and to this day there are regular firesweeps of the lower levels to ensure that they do not once again grow sufficient in number to threaten the hive.

TALLARN DESERT RAIDERS

Tallarn Desert Raiders are mobile guerrilla fighters, evasive and opportunistic. They are masters of hit-and-run warfare, striking a killing blow at the heart of an enemy formation before returning to their own lines, prepared to pounce once more. The people of Tallarn are extremely resourceful and pragmatic. They are patient, determined and utterly ferocious in pursuit of their enemies.

The once fertile planet of Tallarn was all but destroyed during the Horus Heresy when the Iron Warriors Chaos Space Marine Legion launched a surprise attack upon the planet. Thousands of virus bombs rained down upon the surface of Tallarn, and many of its people died whilst attempting to escape the devastation. When the surviving populace emerged from enviro-shelters hidden deep beneath the surface weeks later, their world was unrecognisable, the deadly attack leaving it a barren, desolate wasteland. The Iron Warriors then launched an invasion onto the planet, but instead of a dead world, the traitors encountered fierce resistance from the remaining Tallarns. Residues of the lethal virus that ravaged Tallarn were still present on the world's surface, making it virtually impossible for infantry to operate outside of protective shelters. 'The Battle for Tallarn', as this conflict would be later known, was therefore the largest tank engagement in Imperial history. Vast reinforcements were directed to Tallarn by both sides, enormous resources squandered fighting over a devastated world of no notable strategic worth. During the months that followed the Chaos invasion, more than ten million armoured units clashed over the shifting dunes of Tallarn's blasted surface. The Desert Raiders rarely met the invaders in open battle, preferring to strike from the flanks and dodging the strongest elements of the Chaos battleline. To this day, the Tallarn Desert Raiders have a well-deserved reputation for armoured warfare, and their tank crews are amongst the most feared in the galaxy.

Over the following centuries the final remnants of the virus expired, but Tallarn was irrevocably changed. Deserts of sulphurous sand now stretched from pole to pole, and all water had disappeared except for a thin layer in the atmosphere. No vegetation and few animals remained on the wind-swept surface. The Tallarns lived, as they continue to do, in domed towns or caverns hollowed from the planet's rock where they are protected from the corrosive sandstorms that can strip a man's flesh from his bones. Tall vapour traps were constructed, chanelling what water could be extracted into subterranean holding tanks. A complex system of tunnels were eventually built to facilitate travel between domes and the Desert Raiders are just as apt at fighting over the exposed surface of a planet as they are in the confines of caverns and tunnels.

> "Be swift and silent – as the breeze that crosses the dunes without stirring a grain of sand."
>
> Captain Al'rahem

Tallarns are accomplished riders, using swift mounts to move from battle to battle, dismounting only when they are close to the enemy and wish to employ stealth. Once the enemy are sighted the warriors of Tallarn will stalk them, relying on their practiced marksmanship to achieve victory.

The people of Tallarn are master craftsmen and their wargear is both practical and ceremonial. Indeed, the weapons of many Tallarn officers are inset with precious gems and metals. These officers are usually selected from amongst Tallarn's tribal leaders and a coloured sash tied around every soldier's waist denotes his rank.

Battlegroup 'Desert Fox'

Battlegroup 'Desert Fox' was a composite unit based around the infantry of the 95th Tallarn, the tanks of the 668th Tallarn Armoured, and the mobile guns of the 212th Tallarn Artillery. The formation was constituted to wage war in the arid sulphur wastes of Lorthax against a large army of separatists, where it would spearhead Operation Umbrage. Due to an administrative error however, the column was issued without any source of fuel and had no choice but to dismount all of its vehicle crews and start the attack as light infantry. Reverting to the desert fighting traditions of Tallarn, Battlegroup Desert Fox infiltrated the enemy lines and launched an entirely unanticipated attack that proved so successful it pushed twenty kilometres into enemy territory and wiped out the entire separatist high command. Following this great victory, the three regiments were reconstituted as the 1st Tallarn Raiding Regiment, and their vehicles were assigned to other units.

VOSTROYAN FIRSTBORN

Vostroyan regiments have served the Emperor for countless centuries, however they fight to absolve themselves of a terrible shame enacted by their ancestors during the Horus Heresy. At this dark time, Vostroya was ordered to found additional regiments of soldiers. Vostroya was, as it remains today, a factory world providing vital arms and munitions to the Imperium. The Vostroyan government deemed that the sacrifice of manpower in the great smelteries would render their production quotas unattainable. Reasoning that they could better serve by maintaining the work forces and producing the Emperor's weapons of war, Vostroya reluctantly refused the order to raise any extra armies.

> "We shall wage this war with undaunted faith and courage. We shall not take one step back. This is the Emperor's world and we will not surrender it!"
>
> Lord Marshal Toshenko addressing the
> Vostroyan XVI at the Defence of Nimbosa.

In an act of mercy, the Vostroyans were given a chance to atone for their sins and repay their debt to the Emperor. For ten thousand years the Vostroyans have given up the first-born son of every family for service in the Imperial Guard. There are no exceptions to this, even the greatest noble families must comply. However, to the Vostroyans, it is seen as an honour to serve in the Firstborn regiments, for the populace considers the repayment of their debt to be of paramount importance. Their ancient pact drives them onwards, instilling them with a stubbornness, courage and fortitude rarely seen outside the Adeptus Astartes. Vostroyans reserve a disdain for those Imperial Guard regiments they perceive to be less devoted than themselves.

Thanks to the inhospitable climate of Vostroya, the Firstborn regiments are trained in the most adverse of conditions. Amidst the jutting skeletal spars of half-collapsed manufactorums, the wind howling along rust-pocked alleyways, the Firstborn learn the skills of close-quarter combat and strict firing drills.

Vostroya is governed by the Techtriarchs, a curious committee of Adeptus Mechanicus officials and Imperial Commanders. As a result, Vostroyan uniforms tend to incorporate red, the colour of Mars. Bionic replacement and cyber-augmentation are commonplace amongst Vostroyans and many officers voluntarily undergo such surgery.

The weapons carried by the Vostroyan Firstborn regiments are exquisitely crafted pieces, often heirlooms that are passed down through the generations. Hand-carved wooden stocks and precision-tooled barrels replace the utilitarian weaponry of other Imperial Guard regiments.

The right to carry the regimental standard is given only to the fiercest trooper in the regiment. Competitions and duels for the honour are common and those privileged few display their ritual scars as proudly as the banners they carry.

9th Vostroyan Firstborn 'Old Irascibles'

The Old Irascibles earned their name not through a single battle, but through many hundreds. The regiment served for three and a half centuries during the late 41st Millennium, this being made possible because the Firstborn are one of a very few regiments that ship in reinforcements from their home world in order to stay at fighting strength.

The 9th Vostroyan became one of the most veteran formations in Segmentum Obscurus, before finally meeting their match during the Fall of Karak Prime. The Old Irascibles held the city for eighteen months against a splinter fleet of Hive Fleet Moloch, facing a Tyranid swarm that stretched from the base of the curtain walls to the distant horizon. The defenders knew that the freezing chill of winter would weaken the xenos horde, and that the aliens must feed, by taking the city, before temperatures fell too low. The 9th Vostroyan were running desperately low on ammunition and they knew they would not last that long.

Realising they were doomed, the Old Irascibles opened the city's gates, drawing the ravenous horde within. Only when the bulk of the Tyranid swarm had passed into the city did the 9th Vostroyan regiment detonate its nucleonic stack, incinerating the hive, its defenders and an estimated 85% of the Tyranid swarm. With the coming of midwinter, the few surviving Tyranids starved to death and the splinter fleet was entirely defeated.

ARMAGEDDON STEEL LEGION

Mechanised infantry companies are normally quite rare in the Imperial Guard. This is because it is difficult for most Imperial Commanders and Planetary Governors to obtain and maintain enough of the vehicles needed for such a formation. Amongst those rare few regiments that can equip their companies so, the most famous and celebrated are those raised on Armageddon. This hive world is one of the chief manufacturing planets for Chimeras, producing countless numbers for use across the Imperium. The extremely industrialised nature of Armageddon means that a far higher proportion of its regiments are mechanised infantry. It is for this reason that the hive world's regiments are known as Steel Legions. Fully mobile, the Chimera-mounted infantry squadrons of the Steel Legion regiments are capable of overrunning enemy positions with large convoys before the infantry dismount to finish them off.

The ash wastes of Armageddon are filled with corrosive toxins and industrial pollution. Were a man to breathe the air of Armageddon for any extended period his lungs would quickly rot. As such, all members of the Steel Legion wear protective clothing such as trenchcoats, gloves and visors so as to minimise the exposure to their world's polluted atmosphere. Most notably, every trooper carries a rebreather unit capable of filtering out the worst of the airborne poisons. The rebreathers of senior officers are often fashioned in the visage of a grinning skull in an attempt to unnerve the superstitious Orks that have ravaged their war-torn home world in recent years. The Steel Legions reserve a particular hatred for the Orks, who in their lust for war have smashed whole hive cities asunder and whose presence continues to plague Armageddon.

It is not only the Guardsmen who need be protected from Armageddon's noxious environment. All the vehicles employed by the Armageddon Steel Legions are fully enclosed and airtight to safeguard passengers from the acidic and toxic atmosphere as they traverse the great ash wastes. Even the great banners of the Steel Legions are coated in a highly resistant substance that prevents them decaying in the acrid wastelands.

Many of the Steel Legion troopers are drafted from amongst the crammed populations of Armageddon's massive hive cities, where only the ruthless survive the ceaseless and brutal gang wars. Many of the Armageddon underhive's most notorious gangs are conscripted directly into the Imperial Guard, without the need for any additional training – their ruthless skills proving more than adequate.

> "Heroes of Armageddon! You have withstood the evil savagery of the Orks, and they having nothing left for you to fear. So raise high the black banners of vengeance – now is our time."
>
> Commissar Yarrick
> during the Third War for Armageddon.

Armageddon has a massive population and is capable of raising a large number of Imperial Guard regiments. Indeed, at the height of the Second War for Armageddon more regiments were being raised each year from the population of Armageddon than from any two other worlds in the entire Segmentum Solar combined. Most of the Steel Legion regiments that were raised at this time were destroyed during the Second War for Armageddon, but many were re-founded, decades later, when the greenskins returned once more to plunge the beleaguered hive world into an all-consuming fight for survival. The people of Armageddon are therefore no strangers to warfare. They give no quarter and expect none in return.

339th Armageddon Steel Legion 'The Iron Heads'

The 339th earned the title 'Iron Heads' during the battles for the tank forges of Hive Tempestora during the Third War for Armageddon. So massive was the factory that entire battles were fought within, with Leman Russ, Chimeras and Basilisks manoeuvring and firing as they would in the open expanses of Armageddon's ash wastes. At one point, the 339th held a front line demarcated by a long conveyor belt along which vital components for Leman Russ Battle Tanks trundled even as the battle raged all around. At the height of the battle, the entire regiment was mounted up in Chimeras that had just rolled off the production line and had not even had a coat of primer applied. The 339th then made a mechanised assault along the length of the factory, smashing through the Ork lines and pursuing the hated foe out into the polluted ash wastes of Armageddon Prime.

VALHALLAN ICE WARRIORS

The Valhallan Ice Warriors have a reputation for stoicism and dedication to the Emperor. When attacking, they are renowned for combining massed artillery barrages with infantry assault waves. When defending they show dogged determination, even in the face of defeat.

Valhalla was once a temperate paradise of forests and broad fertile plains. All this changed when the planet was struck by a comet of immense size, so massive that it knocked the world from its orbit and raised clouds of dust that blocked out the sun. The temperature plummeted and barely one percent of all life remained; the survivors were forced to build cities deep inside the ice and beneath glaciers, closer to the core of the planet where there was still some modicum of warmth. Valhalla is now nothing more than an inhospitable, frozen world of ice.

Not even an Ork invasion shortly after this disaster was able to blunt the Valhallans' spirit and their grim denial of surrender, despite overwhelming opposition, won them a historic, if bloody victory. Though the planet of Valhalla is no longer an affluent world, the Ice Warrior regiments raised there are famous throughout the Imperium of Man. After destroying the Ork invaders on their own world, Valhallan regiments, in an act of vengeance, joined with other Imperial Guard armies to cleanse the sector of the hated greenskin menace. Always the Valhallans fought with the same austere determination that was displayed by every man, women and child in the defence of the ice-cities of their home world.

To this day, the courage and tenacity the Valhallans display in battle continues to earn them the respect of other regiments from all over the galaxy.

The Valhallans are a stubborn and stern people who refuse to acknowledge their own hardships. They are all but impervious to harsh conditions and have a casual disregard for human life. Due to the overcrowded subterranean habitats on Valhalla, life is cheap. Even the most petty crime carries with it the death sentence. Those that do not serve in the Valhallan military or volunteer to join the Imperial Guard must toil in the dark caverns, cultivating the nutrient slimes that sustain the populace.

> "The Valhallans hate the cold as much as the rest of us, they're just taught that carpin' on about it gets the Commissars all riled..."
>
> Mosstrooper 'Reiv' Daggat of the 17th Drookian Fenguard
> after serving alongside Valhallans.

Valhallan soldiers are expected to carry each and every item they will need to survive. Without their thermally insulated greatcoats and helmets the Guardsmen's blood would freeze within seconds on the arctic surface of Valhalla. The armoured battle tanks and artillery units of Valhalla are uniformly camouflaged in a manner suited to this frozen tundra, and each vehicle proudly displays the name of their home world on their hulls.

Valhallan 1212th 'Cold Bloods'

The Valhallan 1212th 'Cold Bloods' were raised for service in the Eastlight Nebula Wars, but their first battle was almost their last. The logistics train of the army in which the 1212th were serving was woefully overstretched; the result of which being that only one in three of the Ice Warriors could actually be issued with a lasgun. The regiment's first mission saw it force-marching across the frozen, windblasted and highly toxic phosgene flats of Triox. Despite their hardy constitution and specialist wilderness survival skills, only half of the Ice Warriors made it across the flats to assault the traitors' flank. But many of these heroic individuals had recovered the weapons of the fallen and were determined to put them to use. The survivors of the march proved to be the very best Valhalla had to offer, and the enemy was defeated in short order.

ATTILAN ROUGH RIDERS

The fierce Attilan tribes are formed of a proud and aloof people. Regiments raised on Attila consist entirely of Rough Riders and the Imperium recruits some of its most ferocious mounted warriors from this barbaric world. These specialised cavalry regiments are often split and attached to support other Imperial Guard regiments on thousands of distant worlds. Many light years from Attila, the image of a tribesman resplendent in crude furs and braided hair is as familiar as it is frightening.

The planet of Attila has but a single continent that covers almost half of its surface. Between the scorched death lands of the continental centre and the coast of this enormous land mass, are belts of rich savannah, plains of grasslands thousands of miles wide. The bulk of the population has adopted a nomadic life and subsists from herds of gigantic, savage animals. The tribes gather to trade furs, meat and warriors at Khanasan, the world's only permanent settlement, once a year.

The warrior prowess of the Attilans is founded upon a long tradition of inter-tribal fighting. The horse-clans respect only power and a chieftain must demonstrate his might to doubting rivals. The characteristic features of an Attilan warrior are the scars borne upon his cheeks, long knife cuts of white tissue contrasting against his weather-beaten skin.

The Attilans are said to be born in the saddle, for they are amongst the greatest horsemen in the galaxy. An Attilan can ride as naturally as another man can walk and the riders value their steeds more highly than gold. The horses they prefer are, much like the Attilans themselves, thick-set and ill-tempered beasts. In adversity a warrior can even draw some of his mount's blood and drink it to sustain himself, enabling the Rough Riders to operate deep behind enemy lines without supplies.

ELYSIAN DROP TROOPS

The Elysia system and surrounding wilderness space is notorious for its pirates; the many barren moons, gas clouds and asteroid fields providing perfect ambush sites. Through combating this ever-present threat, the Elysian regiments have become well versed in ship-to-ship boarding actions and fighting in concert with orbital support when attacking isolated pirate bases. Famed for their lightning descents in Valkyrie Assault Carriers, Elysian squads often deploy behind enemy lines via rappelling lines and grav-chutes. Drop Troopers are issued with a Type 5 pressure helmet that incorporates pressure equalising equipment and draws air from the trooper's backpack. Elysians carry plenty of spare ammunition and extra wargear, a common practice amongst troopers that operate deep inside hostile territory without chance to resupply.

DEATH KORPS OF KRIEG

The planet of Krieg was laid to waste when rebellion led to a five hundred year campaign of atomic cleansing. Not content with purging their own home world, the Death Korps now seek to martyr themselves for the greater glory of the Imperium. The Death Korps excel in grinding their enemies down in long battles of attrition and their skills at siege warfare are renowned throughout the galaxy. The Death Korps regiments request to fight in the deadliest war-zones and each soldier is equipped accordingly. The Guardsmen of the Death Korps regiments fight without fear of death, disdaining retreat or surrender. This uncompromising nature is reflected in the Krieg troopers' sinister appearance, many soldiers adorning their uniforms and weapons with skulls and other grisly symbols of mortality.

TANITH FIRST AND ONLY

The forest world of Tanith was destroyed shortly after the initial founding of the planet's first three regiments. The only survivors to escape the attack, the Tanith 1st Regiment, carry with them the wilderness skills learnt on their home world, that make them a superb light-infantry regiment. The Guardsmen of the Tanith First and Only regiment wear distinctive camo-cloaks and they are renowned for their expertise at both scouting and infiltration missions. In addition to their normal equipment, each Guardsman is armed with a straight, silver war-knife, unique to the Tanith regiment. Led by the inspirational Colonel-Commissar Ibram Gaunt and drawing new recruits from the worlds they fight to liberate and defend, the reputation of 'Gaunt's Ghosts' continues to grow with each passing victory.

NOTABLE BATTLES OF THE IMPERIAL GUARD

The following list of events gives a few brief details about some of the battles and campaigns involving the armies of the Imperial Guard during the latter part of the 41st Millennium. This collection represents only a tiny fraction of the countless wars fought during this time.

755.M41

The Sabbat Worlds Crusade begins to reclaim Imperial worlds from the foul clutches of Chaos. It is the largest military offensive since the Macharian Conquests. The crusade outlives Warmaster Slaydo, who names the relatively young Macaroth as his successor, an appointment later confirmed by the Departmento Munitorum and the High Lords of Terra. Under Macaroth's guidance the crusade continues and the names of many Imperial Guard regiments are entered unto the Hall of Heroes on Holy Terra.

762.M41

The Catachan MXIV 'Unseen Lurkers', led by Colonel 'Steel Eye' Black, battle against Orks from the Death Skulls clan on the shadow world of Kato. Neither side is able to gain an advantage until Sentinel teams locate and destroy the Orks' Stompa factory, hidden in the depths of the Widow Valley.

777.M41

Spearheaded by the Black Legion, Chaos Space Marine forces exit the Warp at the Cadian Gate. Their advance into the Imperium is slowed by the actions of the Cadians. Imperial Fists Space Marines reinforcement arrive and help the Guard drive the renegades back into the Eye of Terror.

790.M41

Forces of the Vostroyan IX, serving under the command of Graf Toshenko, die to a man defending the factory city of Polia against the forces of Tau Commander Brightsword on Nimbosa. Inspired by their sacrifice, the populace refuses to submit to the Tau notion of 'the Greater Good'.

845.M41

The Dimmamak War escalates after Dark Eldar pirates capture Warmaster Ingenus. In response, a further forty thousand regiments are raised and all high-ranking Imperial Guard officers are assigned personal bodyguards.

857.M41

A surprise assault by the Eldar of the Saim-Hann Craftworld threatens to annihilate the forces of the Mortant VII 'Headhunters' during the Sacking of Colonia. The Eldar retreat after a single squad of Catachan Devils, led by Gunnery Sergeant Harker, emerges from concealed positions and heavy bolter fire kills the warhost's Autarch.

863.M41

The Cadian 423rd, led by the legendary tank ace Knight Commander Pask, rally to engage rearguard elements of the Adamant Fury Titan Legio during the Saint Cyllia Massacre.

870.M41

In a rare instance where regiments from Attila deploy in force, Mogul Kamir leads a decisive three-year offensive against the Necron tomb wardens of Loxar IV. The enemy forces are finally defeated during the ill-fated charge of the Lumen Valley, the largest cavalry charge in the Imperium's recorded history.

883.M41

The Cadian 423rd spearhead the largest armoured assault since the Battle for Tallarn. Over eight thousand tank companies and thirty five super-heavy detachments are annihilated during the near-total destruction of a renegade Titan Legio at the Planus Steppes.

925.M41

Waaagh! Grax descends upon the Ryza system. Regiments are raised from all planets within ten light years, including the worlds of Barac, Ulani, Dulma'lin and Catachan. To meet the additional tithe requirements, the world of Dulma'lin drafts four-fifths of its total populace.

Commander Mordrid van Hordric finally defeats the bulk of the Orks, decades later at the Battle of Desolation Valley.

926.M41 The Dulma'lin Cleansing

A single regiment of Catachan warriors, led by the bombastic Colonel Straken, is the only regiment to survive planetfall on the world of Dulma'lin. Under Straken's orders, the Catachan regiment fight a year-long guerrilla war in the subterranean depths of the planet's caverns, earning a fearsome reputation amongst the Ork tribes.

The decisive moment in the fighting occurs after Catachan scouts locate the centre of the Ork city in a massive underground cavern known as the Mommothian Vault. Straken personally leads a handpicked team of demolitions experts and infiltrates the Ork settlement. The Catachans' presence is detected on the third day of the operation by a roving pack of Squig-hounds and in the ensuing fight Straken accounts for the deaths of at least thirty Orks and a mob of Killa Kans. The Colonel is seriously injured when he drags Ork Warlord Killzkar into the path of a stampeding Squiggoth which tramples them both into the cavern floor. Straken's men succeed in destroying the Vault's primary support stacks and carry the Colonel's broken body to safety before the entire cavern-ceiling collapses and destroys the Ork settlement.

Imperial reinforcements arrive two days later, led by a haughty Purbech officer, High Praetor Osh'preen. The remaining Ork threat, scattered and leaderless, is exterminated within a week. Osh'preen's report to Segmentum Command fails to mention the Catachan II's true involvemnt in the Dulma'lin campaign, citing Straken's regiment as 'uncouth soldiers, little more civilised than the Orks themselves'. Taking complete credit for the cleansing of Dulma'lin, Osh'preen is awarded governorship of the planet as a reward.

The men of the Catachan II are unceremoniously redeployed to the Ulani system. Colonel 'Iron Hand' Straken is tended to by a team of medicae personnel, clinging onto life throughout the journey. He awakes after extensive bionic surgery to find himself surrounded by the enemy, the Catachan II ever standing by to carry out his orders and win yet another war.

927.M41

The renowned armoured siege units of the Hammeront IV, under command of Grand Marshal Lourgant, are wiped out during the Fallaxian Scourging when an army of Daemons overwhelms the Imperium's forces.

928.M41

The Catachan II assist the Ulani defence battalions in search and destroy missions against Ork Kommandos in the planet's polar mountain range.

929.M41

Such is the delay in transmitting information and updating the Administratum's records, that news of the demise of Hammeront IV regiment fails to reach the Departmento Munitorum and Grand Marshal Lourgant is ordered to lead the liberation of the Abraxis Citadel on Prassium.

930.M41

The Catachan XXIV 'Waiting Death' destroys Krakskull's Orks on Arandra V, luring the entire horde into a booby-trapped ravine with 'Baiter Squads'.

931.M41

The Departmento Munitorum charges the Hammeront IV with desertion and, along with Lord General Lourgant, they are all posthumously sentenced to death.

932.M41

Techno Magus Stannum Vir discovers fragments of an STC device on the agri world of Jollov. However, a vanguard tendril of the newly emergent Tyranid Hive Fleet Moloch threatens to consume the world before it can be recovered. At the Techpriest's behest a courageous defence of the planet's spaceport ensues. Elements of Catachan, Mordian, Kanak, Molov and Agathon regiments die to buy enough time for the Adeptus Mechanicus to flee with the invaluable technological relic.

934.M41

Elysian troops drive off Ork Kaptin Blacklaw and his Freebooterz from the Stranthium Orbital Space Docks, ending a decade long blockade by the alien pirates.

935.M41

The offensive on Bren's World falters when Imperial forces from over two-dozen worlds are unable to take the fortifications at Haven's Spire. The Cadian 12th lead the blitz that finally destroys the Spire following the destruction of several void-shield generators by elite Storm Trooper units.

936.M41

The hive world of Derondii withholds its annual tithes and the Krieg Death Korps are deployed to act as the honour guard of a Departmento Munitorum investigation team. After the Imperium officials are hanged, the Krieg deploy in the towering mountains that overlook the primary hive. Several artillery and siege companies begin to bombard the city spires and the inhabitants are mercilessly gunned down as they try to break out from the besieged city. After ten years of relentless shelling, the hive is reduced to naught but rubble and dust, two years after all signs of life from the hive ceased and five years after the hive issued its unconditional surrender.

937.M41

The Cadian 9th devastates Hive Fleet Scarabus at the walls of Fortress Carcasson without loss of a single company.

938.M41

During the Yaquit 27 campaign, Colonel Straken personally leads the Catachan II in the charge at the Battle for Moden's Ridge, exterminating the L'Huraxi invaders despite being outgunned and outnumbered more than ten to one.

939.M41

Ork attacks throughout Segmentum Solar become more frequent. Whilst serving with the 70th Luther McIntyre regiment on the bleak world of V'run, Commissar Yarrick learns the Ork language from a captured greenskin and develops a unique insight into the Ork psyche.

940.M41

The conquest of Atria IV is halted when Imperial forces are unable to take the Palace of Hate. With the arrival of the Catachan XXIII five years later elite sapper units breach the palace walls within the week.

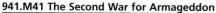

941.M41 The Second War for Armageddon

The Second War for Armageddon begins when Warlord Ghazghkull Mag Uruk Thraka, self proclaimed prophet of the Ork gods Gork and Mork, invades the industrial hive world at the head of the largest Waaagh! ever witnessed.

Commissar Sebastian Yarrick, on Armageddon to assist in the founding of the 4th Armageddon Regiment, recognises in the Warlord a cunning and drive not encountered before in an Ork. Instead of heeding Yarrick's counsel, Herman von Strab, the planet's overlord, banishes 'Old Man' Yarrick to Hades Hive – far from the seat of government.

The savage Ork assault sweeps von Strab's forces aside and only upon reaching Hades Hive do the surging tides falter before the well-ordered defences that Commissar Yarrick put into position. The momentum of the Ork onslaught is stymied during the ensuing Battle for Hades Hive, the Ork Warlord being out-smarted at every turn by Commissar Yarrick and the Orks and Steel Legion defenders reach a bloody standstill.

Hades Hive eventually falls to the Ork invasion and Yarrick is grievously wounded by Ghazghkull himself. The Commissar's stoic defence succeeds in delaying the Warlord long enough for reinforcements to arrive and, spearheaded by three Space Marine Chapters, the back of the Ork Waaagh! is broken. Ghazghkull flees the world to lick his wounds.

Clinging to life, Yarrick is one of the few survivors found in Hades Hive and, soon after his recovery, he is celebrated as the Saviour of Armageddon. Without his leadership, the world of Armageddon and its surrounding systems would surely have been lost to the Orks.

944.M41

Commissar Yarrick comes out of retirement and devotes the remainder of his years to hunting down Ghazghkull and ending the threat he poses to the Imperium forever.

956.M41

The Kieldar Rebellion is utterly crushed by the combined forces of the Cadian, Morax, Loriar, Elysia, Catachan, Aegis, Tallarn, Harkoni, Neocassan, Paragon, Vostroyan, Birmingham, Mordian, Jjojos, Pintax, Athanos, K'phrani, Rassiosan and Bannan regiments.

968.M41

The planet of Khai-Zhan is plunged into rebellion and, led by the Night Lords Traitor Legion, rebels capture every major population centre before daybreak. Less than one-tenth of Imperial Guard regiments sent to retake Khai-Zhan survive. However, in one of the most brutal urban conflicts in recent memory, the Cadian 122nd and their allies succeed in recapturing the capital city of Vogen. With the world's primary starport secured, the Imperium's forces overwhelm the remaining traitors within a month.

975.M41

The young Ursarkar Creed and his Whiteshield squad are hurled into the five-year Drussite Crusade. By the time the Cadian army celebrates its victory in the blaze of the xeno-pyres, Creed has been promoted to Captain.

978.M41

Whilst in the pursuit of his nemesis, Commissar Yarrick is captured at Golgotha. His personal Baneblade, the Fortress of Arrogance, is destroyed during the fighting. He escapes barely a month later in mysterious circumstances, but the planet of Golgotha and its abhuman inhabitants are utterly destroyed by the Orks.

979.M41

The Tau Empire expands into the Imperium's territory and many worlds defect, initiating the protracted Damocles Gulf Crusade in which notable victories are won by the regiments of the Brimlock Dragoons.

980.M41

Chaos Space Marine Lord Brule and his renegades are destroyed on Treconondal by a combined force of the Cadian 8th and Terrax Guard.

983.M41

A Hrud migration is halted due in no small part to the courageous efforts of the Cadian 8th, a campaign in which the tactical abilities of Ursarkar Creed proved instrumental.

988.M41

The Damocles Gulf Crusade is abandoned due to the emergent threat of Tyranid fleet Kraken. The Imperium's forces are redeployed to support other beleaguered worlds.

992.M41

Ursarkar Creed, now Lord General of Cadia destroys the Ulthwé raid on Aurnet.

996.M41

Under the command of the stern taskmaster Kubrik Chenkov, the Valhallan 18th 'Tundra Wolves' wipe out the vanguard of Hive Fleet Jormungandr at Goyan Valley. The swarms of the Tyranids are crushed under the metal treads of Chenkov's armoured brigades and the thundering boots of over a million Guardsmen, driven onto the xenos horde by ruthless Commissars.

998.M41 The Third War for Armageddon

On the day of the Feast of the Emperor's Ascension, fifty seven years to the day after his first invasion of the planet, Ghazghkull Thraka returns to Armageddon, plunging the world into another colossal conflict. Ghazghkull opens the war by completely obliterating Hades Hive from orbit, a clear challenge to his old enemy.

Commissar Yarrick returns once more to oppose the Ork Warlord, this time taking command of the entire world's armed forces. The Fortress of Arrogance is salvaged from ruined Golgotha, and with it Yarrick leads the fight against the Orks.

Though billions lose their lives, Yarrick stops Ghazghkull's hordes from overwhelming Armageddon's major hive cities and the conflict degenerates into a gruelling war of attrition in which neither side can gain a clear advantage. Ghazghkull is himself repulsed from the world and Yarrick once again pursues his nemesis, determined to make the Warlord pay for the death and destruction visited upon Armageddon.

4105999.M41

Reports that a single Catachan Guardsman named Marbo was responsible for the complete destruction of the Ork Gargant *Gorkanought* are dismissed as 'improbable' by Segmentum Command.

3350999.M41

The fiercely uncompromising Colonel Schaeffer leads the 13th Penal Legion – the so-called Last Chancers – into the Daemon World of Fool's Paradise to hunt down the Daemon Prince Mk'Irathirix. Only two survivors return.

3789999.M41

Lord Marshal Graf Harazahn of Vostroya rallies the forces of the Imperial Guard and assumes overall command of the army group. The Lord Marshal's forces defeats the Eldar at the Gates of Balcarhsa.

2975999.M41 The Battle for Tyrok Fields

At the outset of the Despoiler's Thirteenth Black Crusade, treachery strikes at the heart of the Imperium's defences. As defenders of the Cadian Gate muster at Tyrok Fields to salute the Governor Primus, the Volscani Cataphracts reveal their true allegiance - to Chaos. Confusion reigns as defectors and traitors suddenly open fire upon their former comrades, Volscani infiltrators having worked their way into the midst of the Cadian regiments. The traitors slaughter hundreds of loyal Guardsmen before any response can be coordinated. The intent of the Volscani's treason is revealed when they swarm aboard the Leviathan command vehicle of the Governor Primus of Cadia, *Fortress Imperium*, and brutally kill him, leaving the Cadians without a commander-in-chief.

At the darkest moment, Ursarkar Creed, takes control of the situation, rallying the reeling Imperial Guard regiments and organising the counter-attack.

Accompanied as always by his trusted retainer, Jarran Kell, Creed orders the 8th Cadian Regiment to link up with the 7th and advance towards the mutinied Leviathan. Volscani snipers target the standard bearers in an attempt to break the Cadians' morale. The banner of the 7th is carried forward by no fewer than twelve separate troopers over the course of the charge but not once does it fall to the ground. Kell is wounded when he intercepts a las-round intended for Creed. The grizzled sergeant refuses medical attention and continues onwards.

In an impressive feat of military coordination Creed orders the Cadian 190th and 210th Artillery regiments to pin down the traitors' infantry brigades to prevent a flank charge, whilst the firepower of the 20th Cadian Armoured Companies and Titans of the Legio Ignatum are directed to disable the void shields of the captured Leviathan mere moments before the infantry charge hits home. The *Fortress Imperium* is soon recaptured and the colours of the 8th Cadian Regiment are hoisted on the command deck.

Through Creed's actions, what might have been a nefarious victory for the hordes of Chaos, is turned into a defining victory for the defenders of Cadia. Ursarkar Creed is named 'Lord Castellan of Cadia' and the Cadian 8th are renamed 'The Lord Castellan's Own' in his honour.

3978999.M41

The Armageddon 45th Heavy Artillery Regiment decimate the Ork hordes on Minerva. Upon each of the shells fired by the mighty siege weapons is inscribed the name of one of the martyrs of Hades Hive. The Guardsmen of the Heavy Artillery Regiment believe by doing so, the spirits of these brave warriors will have some measure of vengeance against the Emperor's enemies.

3982999.M41

The Mordian 56th proves instrumental in defeating the rebels during the Komarl Revolt. The Iron Guard regiment executes ten percent of the remaining population for failing in their duty to the Emperor. The fear of further reprisals from the Mordian garrison left on Komarl ensures no additional further recidivism.

5985999.M41

Several Catachan regiments mount a protracted campaign of guerilla attacks on the world of Cytheria after its governor defects to the Tau Empire. Snipers from the Catachan LI 'Black Vipers' eliminate a prominent Tau leader, striking a critical blow to the alien's morale.

6990999.M41

Ornsworld comes under attack from the Knights of Blood Chaos Space Marines renegades. In a cruel repetition of the horrors inflicted during the Gothic War, over ninety percent of its population is massacred before Imperial Guard reinforcements arrive to bolster the beleaguered planet.

A GALAXY AT WAR

The Imperial Guard is the Imperium's largest fighting force. As such, it would be impossible to show even a small percentage of their actions. This map therefore shows only the most notable Imperial Guard campaigns and home worlds at 997.M41.

Kaledon

Treconandal

Dimmamar

Jollov

9

Kanak

Coronis Agathon

SEGMENTUM OBSCURUS

Cyris

Krandor

5

Vostroya

Ornsworld

Khai-Zhan

Cypra Mundi

Valhalla

Mordian

Prassrum

6

Fool's Paradise

Belis Corona

GOTHIC SECTOR

Orana

Ogris Major

18

Hammeront

HALO STARS

Cadia

Volscar

Aumet

2

Jjojos

Mahr'douk

Armageddon

Molov

Bren's World

Elysia

Hyrdaphur

SEGMENTUM PACIFICUS

Minerva

Arandra V

14

Harkon

1

Golgotha

SEGMENTUM SOLAR

20

Drondii

The Ryza Warzone

Macharia

Banna

10

Thoth

Gathalamor

3

Atria IV

Ultima Macharia

16

Octavia

15

Extent of the Macharian Conquests

UHULIS SECTOR

Luther McIntyre

Krieg

Balor

Pintax

Tallarn

Vhun

17

Jurn

Jorn V

The Athonian 5th Army Group pursues Waaagh! Killfang

11

Mortant

SEGMENTUM TEMPESTUS

REDUCTUS SECTOR

7

Athanos

Esko

Bakka

San Leo

The 'Pax Imperium', a Mars class battlecruiser, was the first flagship of Lord Solar Macharius for five years until its near destruction at the Battle for Charaxdis.

Gryphonne IV

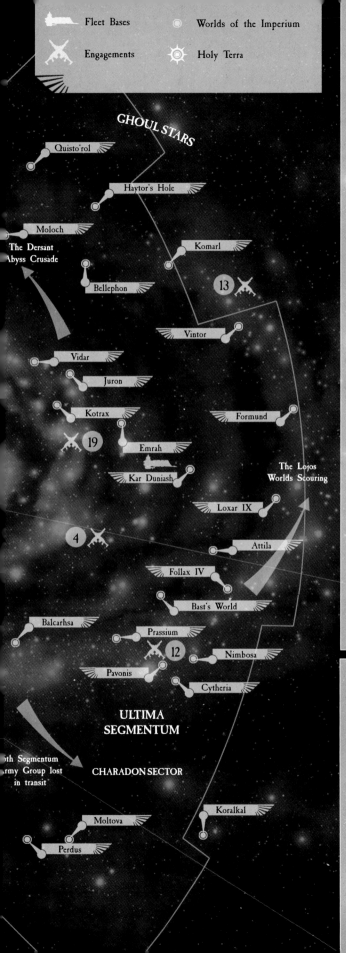

Legend

- Fleet Bases
- Engagements
- Worlds of the Imperium
- Holy Terra

GHOUL STARS

Quisto'rol
Haytor's Hole
Moloch
The Dersant Abyss Crusade
Komarl
Bellephon
Vintor
Vidar
Juron
Kotrax
Formund
Emrah
Kar Duniash
Loxar IX
The Lojos Worlds Scouring
Attila
Follax IV
Bast's World
Balcarhsa
Prassium
Nimbosa
Pavonis
Cytheria

ULTIMA SEGMENTUM

...th Segmentum ...rmy Group lost in transit

CHARADON SECTOR

Koralkal
Moltova
Perdus

NOTABLE ONGOING ENGAGEMENTS 997.M41

1. The Red Corsairs descend upon the Dentor system slaughtering millions. Over one hundred new regiments are raised.

2. Abaddon the Despoiler launches his 13th Black Crusade upon the Imperium. All available Imperial army groups are redirected towards the Cadian Gate. Lord Castellan Ursarkar Creed of Cadia under overall command.

3. The Octavius War escalates as several Eldar warhosts enter the fray, laying waste to both Imperial and Ork forces. No reinforcements available due to Hive Fleet Leviathan containment strategy.

4. The Targus Home Warden force is all but wiped out in the onslaught of Waaagh! Skullkrak. Request for reinforcements pending Administratum feasibility study.

5. Chaos Renegades raid the Gothic Sector. One hundred and fifty additional Imperial Guard regiments to be raised.

6. Grand-Marshal Durov of Vostroya reports daemonic incursions in the Final Sector. Contact with Durov's army group now lost, whereabouts unknown.

7. Army Group Twelve, comprised mainly of Catachan and Jornian forces, continue to hold out against a tendril of Hive Fleet Leviathan. Reinforcements being raised.

8. The Valhallan 812th continue to defend the forge world of M'khan from the Iron Warriors siege. Heavy casualties, victory imminent.

9. Led by the Mordian General Eisen, Imperial reinforcements, make planet fall on Cilix and begin a systematic purge to rid the world of Ork infestation. Resistance high.

10. Catachan regiments rout the forces of the Alaitoc Craftworld from the mining world of Fortuse III. Techpriests dispatched to investigate arcane ruins discovered by Catachan scout teams.

11. Rebellion on Skaroth is crushed by regiments from Pintax, Tallarn and Luther McIntyre. Casualties are heavier than anticipated.

12. The Tau Empire continues its third phase of expansion into the Imperium. All nearby worlds ordered to increase their military tithe contributions to at least twenty percent.

13. The Tollovian Cluster campaign continues under the command of Sub-overlord Ven Vambold. Distinctions won by several Imperial Guard regiments.

14. Cadian 122nd Armoured Regiment leads the counter-attack on Excovar against Waaagh! Bigtoof. Current projections indicate that the greenskins should be repelled by the end of .M42.

15. Dark Eldar raids on the abhuman world of Chogros continue. Catachan, Atrian and Katon regiments engaged in search and destroy missions.

16. Bombardment of the heavily-shielded Wrath's Spire by the Krieg 786th and Loriar 273rd regiments continues. Use of Deathstrike Missiles authorised.

17. Tallarn regiments engage Necron Monoliths on Dreska. Storm Trooper reinforcements en route.

18. Elysian and Harakoni regiments dispatched to investigate communications loss in the Antorro system. Reports show that the Space Hulk *Agony of the Damned* has been sighted in the system.

19. The Emrah battle-fortress is reactivated by forces unknown. First army group wave annihilated. Cadian super-heavy detachments recalled from the Vidar system to lead the second wave and engage the threat.

20. Decades on from the initial onslaught of Waaagh! Grax, Orks continue to enter the Ryza system. Response zone increased to match secondary Ork threats.

Ryza Warzone: Ork Invasion

56–Z655/5/8/77 Ultima Segmentum

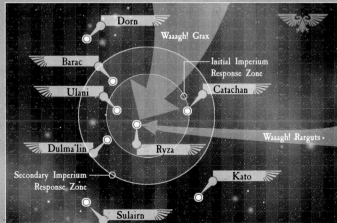

Dorn
Waaagh! Grax
Barac
Initial Imperium Response Zone
Ulani
Catachan
Dulma'lin
Ryza
Waaagh! Rarguts
Secondary Imperium Response Zone
Kato
Sulairn

FORCES OF THE IMPERIAL GUARD

This section of the book details the forces used by the Imperial Guard – their weapons, their units and some famous special characters that you can choose to use, such as Colonel 'Iron Hand' Straken or Commissar Yarrick, the Hero of Hades Hive and saviour of Armageddon. Each entry describes the unit and gives the specific rules you will need to use them in your games of Warhammer 40,000. The army list given later refers to the page numbers of these entries, so you can check back as you pick your force.

The Forces of the Imperial Guard section is sub-divided into two parts. The first part describes all of the troops and vehicles fielded by the Imperial Guard, including the special characters, while the second part details the Imperial Guard's armoury of weapons and equipment.

Special Rules

The models in an Imperial Guard army use a number of special rules. Where those rules are unique to a particular troop type, they are detailed in that unit's bestiary entry. Any special rules that are not explained in the unit's bestiary entry can be found in the Warhammer 40,000 rulebook.

Unique Equipment

The army list at the back of the book shows all the standard and optional wargear available to a particular model. You will find some items of equipment are unique to particular characters or units, while others are used by more than one unit. When an item is unique, it is detailed in the entry for its owning unit; otherwise it is detailed in the wargear section.

Heavy Weapons Teams

The army list at the back of the book refers to models known as Heavy Weapons Teams. Imperial Guard heavy weapons are typically crewed by a team of two men. Generally speaking, one crewman carries and fires the weapon while the other carries the ammunition. A Heavy Weapons Team counts as two models for the purposes of transport capacity but otherwise is treated as a single model.

Vehicle Squadrons

The Imperial Guard can field a number of vehicles in squadrons. These include, amongst other things, Leman Russ Battle Tanks. Such units follow all the rules for vehicle squadrons as detailed in the Warhammer 40,000 rulebook.

IMPERIAL GUARD ORDERS

The ranks of the Imperial Guard are not trained to think independently or to use their initiative, relying instead on their officers for guidance and direction. To this end, Imperial Guardsmen are conditioned to obey orders without question or hesitation. Only by concentrating on their orders to the exclusion of all else can a common trooper override thoughts of self-preservation and face the horrors of the galaxy. A rigid chain of command exists from the commander of a battle group down to the lowliest trooper.

A number of models in the Imperial Guard army have the ability to issue one or more orders each turn. These models are known as officers. Each officer's entry will clearly state the number and type of orders he can attempt to issue, as well as his command radius – the maximum range of his orders.

Orders must be issued at the start of the Shooting phase and in a strict order, representing the Imperial Guard's chain of command. Officers in Company Command squads must issue their orders first. Once all Company Command officers have issued their orders, officers in Platoon Command squads can attempt to issue their own orders.

An officer may attempt to issue orders provided that he is not locked in an assault, embarked in a transport vehicle, falling back or has gone to ground. Orders must be issued before the officer and his Command Squad shoot or run. Issuing orders (whether the order was successful or not) does not prevent an officer and his Command Squad from shooting or running.

To issue an order the officer must declare which order he is attempting to use and select a single friendly non-vehicle unit within his command radius to carry out the order. This can be the officer's own squad if you wish. The chosen unit must then take a Leadership test to see if the order has been

understood and acted upon. Orders cannot be issued to squads that are embarked in a transport vehicle, or units that have already run, made a shooting attack or have already received an order that turn (whether or not the prior order was successful). Unless otherwise stated, orders cannot be issued to units that are falling back or have gone to ground.

Orders Received, Sir!

If the test is passed, the officer's men leap to obey without hesitation – the squad immediately carries out the order and may not act further during the Shooting phase. Once the order has been completed, the officer can attempt to issue another order (if he is eligible to do so). When the officer has finished issuing orders, he and his Command Squad can shoot/run normally if the player wishes.

Inspired Tactics

If a double 1 is rolled for the order, the officer has enforced his will in record time. Once the order has been completed, the officer can immediately issue a further order (there is no need to make a test). This additional order is 'free' and does not count towards the number of orders the officer can issue in a turn.

Could You Repeat That, Sir?

If the test is failed, there has been a breakdown of communications. The order does not take effect, although both the officer's squad and the ordered squad may otherwise act normally in the Shooting phase.

Incompetent Command

If a double 6 is rolled for the order, confusion reigns. Not only does this order not take effect, as described above, but no further orders can be issued (by any officer) in this Shooting phase.

COMPANY COMMAND SQUAD

The most senior officer of an Imperial Guard company leads his troops as part of a Command Squad. The Company Command Squad is the heart of an Imperial Guard army, directing the actions of specific units, disseminating orders and executing the commander's battle strategy with ruthless efficiency. Command Squads typically number five men, the officer assisted by the regiment's most competent soldiers. They are often given additional training and equipment, enabling them to function as combat medics, vox-operators and other orderlies. Often, a soldier who has displayed gallantry above and beyond the call of duty is inducted into the Command Squad. Such a trooper may be permitted to carry the regimental standard, a privileged distinction that reminds the company to fight with duty and honour.

Officers are drawn from the same planet as their regiment and the method by which such men are appointed depends very much upon the culture of their home world. Some commanders are schooled through war academies, drawn only from noble families or blood lines. On other planets only the strongest or most savage may rule, leadership is ascertained through trials of skill and combat. A rare few officers are those who have worked their way up through the ranks, survivors of a dozen campaigns and as many field promotions. The Tactica Imperialis normally uses specific titles to refer to these ranks; Company Commanders for example are most commonly referred to as captains. In practice however, the Imperial Guard is drawn from so many different worlds, many of which speak varying dialects – or even totally different languages – that the actual titles applied to can vary wildly. Major, byzarr, hetman, spear-chief, prime-warden and high praetor are all broadly equivalent titles. Many Imperial Guard officers share a noble ideology of duty to the Emperor and the defence of the Imperium. Others are ambitious and see their position as a stepping stone to power, glory, honour or a death worthy of a hero.

Leading by example, Company Commanders fight on the front line where they provide a solid anchor of leadership. For them and their men, the battle is won or lost at the sharp end of a lasgun's bayonet.

	WS	BS	S	T	W	I	A	Ld	Sv
Company Commander	4	4	3	3	3	3	3	9	5+
Veteran	3	4	3	3	1	3	1	7	5+
Veteran Weapons Team	3	4	3	3	2	3	2	7	5+

Special Rules

Senior Officer: The Company Commander can issue up to two orders each turn. He has a command radius of 12". Company Commanders can use the *Bring It Down!*, *Fire on my Target!* and *Get Back in the Fight* orders described below, as well as the *First Rank, FIRE! Second Rank, FIRE!*, *Incoming!* and *Move! Move! Move!* orders described on page 36.

Bring it Down! Enemy war engines (and alien monsters) are a high priority amongst commanders, who know full well the carnage they can wreak.

If the order is successfully issued, choose one enemy vehicle (or squadron of vehicles) or monstrous creature (or unit of monstrous creatures) visible to the officer. The ordered unit immediately shoots at the nominated target, counting their weapons as twin-linked.

Fire on my Target! Assisted by orbital relays, targeting matrices or just a good pair of binoculars, the officer coordinates firepower onto the enemy's weakpoints.

If the order is successfully issued, choose one enemy unit visible to the officer. The ordered unit immediately shoots at the nominated target. Successful cover saves taken against this shooting attack must be re-rolled.

Get Back in the Fight! A fleeing squad regroups and goes to battle once again, more afraid of their officer than all of the enemy's fearsome weapons.

This order can only be issued to a unit that is falling back, or that has gone to ground. If the order is successfully issued, the ordered unit immediately regroups if falling back (even if it would not normally be able to do so due to casualties suffered, enemy proximity and so on…) or returns to normal (if it had gone to ground). As a result, the ordered squad may shoot and assault as normal this turn.

REGIMENTAL ADVISORS

The commander of an Imperial Guard army is assisted by a host of orderlies, adjutants, aides de camps and specialist advisors from outside the regiment who are able to liaise with other elements of the battle group.

Astropaths serve in the Imperial Guard as planetary communicators. They can transmit and receive covert orders and other sensitive information. In addition, many Astropaths also have mystic powers of divination. Accordingly these psykers can advise Imperial Guard officers how best to guide and redeploy their own forces. Astropaths are easily distinguished by their hooded robes and sunken, empty eye sockets. Most Astropaths are blind and many have lost other sensory perceptions as a result of the traumatic Soul Binding ritual; however, their increased psychic talents tend to make up for any loss of sight.

Attempts by Company Commanders to call down close-ranged artillery fire can result in disastrous casualties amongst the Imperial Guard. Whilst the loss of life is regrettable, the waste of ammunition is intolerable. Masters of Ordnance are therefore attached to Command Squads. These artillery experts have all manner of auspex ident-arrays, range finding bionic implants and modified servo-skulls that rove ahead of the main advance and pinpoint specific targets. The Master of Ordnance communicates directly with his counterparts in artillery companies, relaying the location of enemy forces, calling down a deadly bombardment with an accuracy not otherwise possible.

It is standard procedure to attach an Officer of the Fleet as a liaison to commanders on the ground. Officers of the Fleet are proud, aloof and stern men. They coordinate with Imperial Navy bomber wings and even the lance batteries onboard warships. Whilst the full might of the Imperial Fleet cannot be called upon, the available firepower is enough to disrupt the enemy's supply lines, forcing their reserves to take shelter or face destruction from above. Such actions delay enemy reinforcements from entering the fray, allowing the Imperial Guard to annihilate the foe one unit at a time.

Not all specialists are attached to a Command Squad in an advisory capacity. Bodyguards are battle-scarred warriors and amongst the most devoted warriors of the regiment. The means by which a soldier is granted this task depends upon the regiment's culture. Some are sworn retainers who have protected their master since birth, others have earned the honour as a reward for years of exemplary service. They are tasked with but a single duty, protecting the life of the Company Commander – no matter the cost. Bodyguards are sombre individuals who stand ever ready to intercept an assassin's blade or hurl themselves in the line of fire.

Special Rules

Telepathic Relay: Whilst the Astropath is alive, you add 1 to any of your reserve rolls. In addition, if any of your units arrive using the outflank rule, you can re-roll the dice used to determine which board edge these squads arrives from.

Artillery Bombardment: This is treated as a shooting attack made by the Master of Ordnance, with the following profile:

Range	Strength	AP	Type
Unlimited	9	3	Ordnance Barrage 1*

If a hit is rolled, the template scatters 2D6" in the direction shown by the arrow on the 'Hit' symbol. If an arrow is rolled, the template scatters an additional D6" (for a total deviation of 3D6"). In either case, if the Master of Ordnance has line of sight to his target he then reduces the total distance scattered by his Ballistic Skill. This attack cannot be made if the Master of Ordnance moved in the preceding Movement phase.

Intercept Reserves: Whilst the Officer of the Fleet is alive, your opponent must subtract 1 from all of his reserve rolls. In addition, if any enemy units arrive using the outflank rule, you may choose to make your opponent re-roll the dice used to determine which board edge these squads arrives from.

Look Out – Arghh! Whilst a Bodyguard is alive, each time the Command Squad is wounded by the enemy, up to two wounds allocated to the Company Commander are instead resolved against the Bodyguard(s).

	WS	BS	S	T	W	I	A	Ld	Sv
Astropath	3	4	3	3	1	3	1	7	5+
Master of Ordnance	3	4	3	3	1	3	1	7	5+
Officer of the Fleet	3	4	3	3	1	3	1	7	5+
Bodyguard	4	4	3	3	1	3	2	7	5+

COMMISSARS

Commissars are ruthless and courageous individuals. Rigid adherents to the Imperial Creed, their dedication to the service of the Emperor overrides any feelings of compassion, mercy or common humanity for the men they must lead in battle. Universally feared, and often hated by those around them, Commissars have the power to summarily execute any trooper or officer found wanting on the field of battle. It is a Commissar's duty to maintain the morale, discipline and fighting spirit of the regiment, and to punish cowardice and incompetence wherever it is found. The knowledge that a Commissar is looking over their shoulder for the slightest lapse focuses the minds of the Guardsmen considerably. Such is their reputation that in some regiments the wrath of the Commissar is more feared than the enemy.

Many Commissars first serve in one of the elite Storm Trooper companies and as such are well versed in the tactics and brutality of warfare. They despise the Emperor's enemies and desire nothing more than the chance to crush the foe beneath the righteous heel of the Imperium's might.

Commissars are fanatically brave and their devotion to the Imperium is utterly without doubt. They personify the ideals of loyalty to one's comrades and to the Emperor. Commissars are brooding and remote figures. To denote their rank, they wear distinctive black dress uniforms, long overcoats and peaked caps proudly displaying Imperium insignia.

High-ranking officers of the Departmento Munitorum, Commissars provide the link between regimental officers and strategic command. At least one Commissar is assigned to every regiment, and most will have several who remain with the regiment throughout its duties. Unlike individual regiments that are levied from their home worlds when they are needed, Commissars are raised in the Schola Progenium. It is the Commissars who supervise the raising of new regiments, many of which come from savage worlds where warriors are ill-disciplined and respect only strength and fighting prowess. The loyalty of such troops must be earned, so Commissars are always prepared to demonstrate their courage and skills in battle.

Commissars lead by example and are the first to step up to the firing line to repel an enemy attack, each levelling their bolt pistol with calm assurance. Unwavering and resolute, a Commissar's uncompromising code of honour and defiance of corruption stands as an illustration to all nearby troops, inspiring them to feats they would not have dreamt possible.

The gallantry of Lord Commissars is legendary and tales abound of stranded, demoralised Imperial Guard squads being driven to valorous deeds by the leadership of such heroes. Lord Commissars exemplify power and bravery, making them natural leaders with a reputation for turning the tide of battle, snatching victory from the jaws of defeat.

	WS	BS	S	T	W	I	A	Ld	Sv
Commissar	4	4	3	3	1	3	2	9	5+
Lord Commissar	5	5	3	3	3	3	3	10	5+

Special Rules

Stubborn: Commissars bestow the Stubborn special rule on any unit they have joined or are part of.

Summary Execution: If the Commissar's unit fails a Morale test the Commissar will summarily execute the squad's current commander – this is the model in the squad with the highest Leadership value.

If two or more models in the same squad as the Commissar have the same Leadership value, randomly determine which of the models is executed. A Commissar (of either rank) will never execute himself or another Commissar (of either rank) – ignore these models when determining who is eligible for execution.

The executed model is immediately removed as a casualty, regardless of number of Wounds remaining. The unit in question must then re-roll the failed Morale check – if this test also fails then the squad falls back as normal.

Independent Character (Lord Commissar Only)

Aura of Discipline (Lord Commissar only): Any friendly unit within 6" of a Lord Commissar may use his Leadership of 10 for any Morale or Pinning tests as well as Leadership tests incurred by orders issued to the squad.

PRIMARIS PSYKERS

Primaris Psykers are rare and extraordinary individuals who wield the destructive power of the Warp as a weapon to smite the enemies of the Emperor. With a single thought the psyker conjures forth lightning that leaps from his hands and surrounds his body. With a gesture the psyker hurls these bolts of ether-energy at his opponents, burning the foes' synapses and searing their flesh from their bones.

Mysterious and aloof, Primaris Psykers, also known as primary-psykers, battle-psykers or psyker-lords, are treated with a mixture of awe and fear, but most of all, suspicion by the superstitious soldiers of the Imperial Guard. Their presence is utterly abhorrent to some commanders and they are at best mistrusted. However, their ability to combat the blasphemous magicks of aliens and heretics usually outweighs the natural revulsion to the inclusion of psykers into the ranks of the Imperial Guard.

A Primaris Psyker is typically attached to a high-ranking Imperial Guard officer who can direct the psyker's powers as the situation necessitates, providing psychic support to the troopers on the front line. A battle-psyker marches to war in a uniform daubed with wards and sigils of power. A Primaris Psyker carries a staff made of rare woods and precious metals that can channel the psychic energy of the wielder. A psyker can focus his prodigious mental strength through such a psycho-reactive staff, transforming it into a searing weapon that glows with a barely contained, otherworldly power capable of cutting through reinforced ceramite and ripping the life force from those it strikes.

Of all the psykers judged under the uncompromising gaze of the Inquisition, only those whose mental fortitude is great enough have the merest glimmer of hope of becoming a Primaris Psyker in the Imperial Guard. Battle-psykers are by no means the most powerful of their kind, but even so, they walk a fine line between service to the Emperor and eternal damnation. Every time they unleash their powers they risk predation from the denizens of the Warp; daemonic entities swarm to their bright psyker-soul like moths to a flame. Several fail-safes are therefore built into a psyker's wargear. Complex micro-circuitry and neuro-active wiring are connected to psychically attuned crystals embedded in a psyker's hood or collar, designed to bleed away excess Warp-energy. Such precautions are not limited to the psyker's wargear alone and most have undergone cranial surgeries to implant neural inhibitors that limit the danger of possession – however such actions tend to blunt the psyker's innate power as well. When combined with a lifetime of training a Primaris Psyker has a reasonable chance of avoiding powerful psychic enemies and resisting daemonic influences. For those who prove to be too weak, however, there is always the final safeguard, in the shape of the smoking muzzle of a Commissar's bolt pistol.

	WS	BS	S	T	W	I	A	Ld	Sv
Primaris Psyker	4	4	3	3	2	3	3	9	5+

Special Rules
Independent Character, Psyker.

It's For Your Own Good: If a Primaris Psyker suffers a Perils of the Warp attack whilst joined to the same unit as a Commissar (of any type) then the psyker is immediately executed and removed as a casualty.

Psychic Powers
Lightning Arc: Focusing his mind, the psyker unleashes a roiling burst of Warp lightning upon the foe.

This is a psychic shooting attack with the following profile:

Range	Strength	AP	Type
24"	6	5	Assault 2D6

Nightshroud: The psyker reaches into the minds of his foe, obscuring himself and his companions from the sight of the enemy.

This power is used at the start of the psyker's Movement phase. If successful, any unit wishing to shoot at the psyker (or the unit he is with) must first pass a Leadership test or forego their Shooting phase (vehicles count as Leadership 10 for the purposes of the Nightshroud). The effects of this power last until the beginning of the Primaris Psyker's next Movement phase.

TECHPRIEST ENGINSEERS

The presence of Techpriest Enginseers is vital for the Imperial Guard's regiments' armoured units to function effectively. Adeptus Mechanicus personnel serve as the custodians of the vehicles attached to an Imperial Guard force, preparing the equipment for battle. Many Techpriests carry incense burners and, through painstaking mystic rites and ceremonies, attempt to ward away data-corrupting influences. By intoning intricately phrased chants, and applying meticulously prepared oils and unguents, the methodical Techpriests sanctify Mankind's weapons with the blessings of the Machine God.

On the battlefield the red-robed Techpriest Enginseers are clad in power armour to protect them whilst they tend to their duties. Techpriest Enginseers use the arcane lore of technology to effect battlefield repairs to the damaged fighting machines of the Imperial Guard. The logic-driven Techpriests are utterly focused on their task, and willingly enter the fray when a valuable piece of technology is threatened. They smite their enemies with sweeps of double-handed wrench-axes and crush their foes with hydraulically driven servo-arms capable of hefting giant armour plates or crushing a man's bones to dust with equal ease.

Techpriest Enginseers may be aided in their ministrations by lobotomised Servitors – task-adapted slaves of living flesh and mechanical components designed to perform a single laborious function to the exclusion of all else. There are untold billions of these mindless, mono-tasked cyborgs throughout the Imperium of Man, many working in hostile atmospheres where an unmodified human body would quickly perish. Servitors are not even considered to be as valuable as the engraved and gilded constructs of servo-skulls, which are typically created from the cranial remains of a favoured servant of the Emperor. Servitors are truly the lowest form of bio-mechanical life.

The highest-ranking tech-adepts are known as the Magi. They are powerful individuals in the Priesthood of Mars who are dedicated to the recovery and preservation of lost knowledge. Some Magi have been known to requisition entire armies to recover such knowledge, whether it be a revered relic harking back to the Dark Age of Technology, or the tiniest fragment of a machine's memory core. The calculating adept will sacrifice many lives to ensure the retrieval of such treasured prizes.

The degree of bionic augmentation and cybernetic replacement the adepts of the Machine Cult will have undergone is commensurate with the Techpriests' length of service and position within the Adeptus Mechanicus. The most ancient members of the Cult of Mars are more machine than man, flesh and blood replaced with cold steel and hydraulic oil.

	WS	BS	S	T	W	I	A	Ld	Sv
Techpriest Enginseer	3	3	3	3	1	3	1	8	3+
Servitor	3	3	3	3	1	3	1	8	4+

Special Rules

Blessings of the Omnissiah: A Techpriest in base contact with a damaged vehicle in the Shooting phase can attempt to repair it instead of firing, unless he is falling back or has gone to ground. Roll a D6 and add 1 for each Servitor with a servo-arm in the unit. If the result is a 5 or more, then a Weapon Destroyed or an Immobilised result (owning player's choice) is repaired. If a Weapon Destroyed result is repaired, that weapon can be fired in the following Shooting phase.

Mindlock: The altered and fragmented brain of a Servitor functions poorly unless constantly supervised.

Unless led by a Techpriest, a unit containing Servitors must roll a D6 at the start of each friendly turn. If the result is a 1, 2 or 3 the unit may not move, shoot or assault that turn, though it will fight in close combat if already engaged.

Wargear

Servo-arm: Servo-arms are capable of lifting incredible loads or crushing those that get too close.

A servo-arm grants a model an additional close combat attack that strikes at Initiative 1, Strength 8 and ignores armour saves.

MINISTORUM PRIESTS

The Priests of the Ecclesiarchy play a vital role in the Imperial Guard, imparting the holy teachings of the Emperor and providing spiritual succour to the troops both on and off the battlefield. To these Priests there is no calling higher than tending the Emperor's armies. They lead by example and gladly martyr themselves on blood-soaked fields, the highest sacrifice that is expected of them. Some Ministorum Priests are particularly noted for their fiery zeal in the execution of both their duties and of the heretics they abhor.

More than one Imperial Commander has been grateful for the powerful oratory of a Ministorum Priest. Their fiery speeches can stir a populace to rebel against a heretic lord or persuade an army to lay down its arms and surrender to the mercy of the Emperor – which is inevitably quick and bloody.

All members of the Ecclesiarchy will take with them a rosarius – a symbol of faith as potent as the holy Aquila. The more bloodthirsty of Ministorum Priests, including those that have ties to the redemption cults, often preach in the swirling melee of combat, backing up their battlefield sermons with gouts of cleansing fire and sweeping arcs of roaring chainblades.

Ministorum Priests ensure that the troops are sufficiently motivated to do their duty without fear, as well as fighting fanatically themselves. In battle they harness the faith of the troops to smite the Emperor's foes. Chanting litanies of devotion and mantras of hate, the hearts and souls of nearby Guardsmen are filled with righteous anger. Together they charge down the heretical forces that dare oppose the Emperor, determined to purge such filth from the battlefield.

> "No army is big enough to conquer the galaxy. But faith alone can overturn the universe."
>
> Ecclesiarch Deacis IX

The adepts of the Ministorum have many different titles and varied roles, but the specific duties are of importance only to the Priests themselves. To the troopers who look up to these holy individuals such distinctions are purely academic. Indeed, many newly inducted Guardsmen are unable to tell the difference between a humble preacher and an esteemed cardinal. The Priests themselves may not always be from the same home world as the regiment, and they must be able to incorporate and assimilate the different cultural creeds and methods of worship into their own belief system. Everything from primitive sacrificial rituals to formal mantras and prayer are used by the Priests to bolster the faith of the troops.

Confessors are amongst the highest ranking Priests within the Ministorum, and are given carte blanche by the Ecclesiarchy to preach where they wish. They have no formal diocese, but instead move from world to world rooting out apostates, burning blasphemers, and instilling fervent faith in the locals. Confessors may act as advisors to Imperial officers and occasionally, with Ecclesiarchal dispensation, they initiate Wars of Faith against the Emperor's foes.

	WS	BS	S	T	W	I	A	Ld	Sv
Ministorum Priest	3	3	3	3	1	3	2	7	5+

Special Rules
Independent Character.

Righteous Fury: A Priest and his unit re-roll any failed To Hit rolls in close combat on the turn in which they assault. Righteous Fury has no effect on Ogryns, who are simply confused by the Priest's rhetoric, or Ratlings, who are far too concerned with their own survival.

Wargear
Eviscerator: An eviscerator is a massive two-handed chainsword capable of inflicting horrific damage on living creatures and vehicles alike.

An eviscerator counts as a power fist, but rolls an additional D6 for armour penetration.

Rosarius: A Rosarius is a badge of faith incorporating a powerful conversion field that protects its wearer from harm.

A rosarius grants the bearer a 4+ invulnerable save.

PLATOON COMMAND SQUAD

The Imperial Guard is a vast fighting formation and even basic troop movements can involve the mobilisation of thousands of men. For these operations to go smoothly the Imperial Guard has a substantial command structure. One of the first links in this chain is the Platoon Command Squad.

The officers who lead Platoon Command Squads are known by a variety of official ranks and titles; lieutenant, marshal and shield-centurion are are just a few examples. Their role is to ensure the platoon fulfills the Company Commander's orders and gets the job done. Sadly, for every fresh-faced officer who bravely leads his troops against the enemy there is another who panics and falters in the heat of battle. These incompetent individuals are responsible for wasting countless lives and such ineptitude is quickly punished.

Platoon Commanders are accompanied by a hand-picked team who help him fulfill his duties. Some are chosen for their courage and may be given the honour of carrying the platoon standard. Others are chosen for their technical or medical skills. A select few are individuals that are thought suitable for officer training. Troopers chosen to join the Command Squad not only assist in relaying the officer's orders but also gain first hand leadership experience.

The number of Platoon Command Squads in a regiment varies tremendously. Constant attrition amongst the

regiment's officers, especially those who fight the enemy face-to-face, means that companies must continue to re-organise, almost on a daily basis. It is not surprising therefore that many Platoon Commanders have been commissioned from the rank and file. Field promotions and brevet ranks are commonplace and necessary to ensure that the chain of command remains unbroken.

The Command Squad coordinates ambushes, prioritises targets, positions kill-zones and leads the charge to destroy the enemy. Platoon Commanders bellow orders over the din of war, their call to advance audible even over the cacophony of weapons fire and the screams of dying men.

	WS	BS	S	T	W	I	A	Ld	Sv
Platoon Commander	4	4	3	3	1	3	2	8	5+
Guardsman	3	3	3	3	1	3	1	7	5+
Heavy Weapons Team	3	3	3	3	2	3	2	7	5+

Special Rules

Junior Officer: The Platoon Commander can issue one order each turn. He has a command radius of 6". Platoon Commanders can use the *First Rank, FIRE! Second Rank, FIRE!*, *Incoming!*, and *Move! Move! Move!* orders as described below.

First Rank, FIRE! Second Rank, FIRE! The Guardsmen unleash a fusillade of lasgun volleys into the enemy to the tempo of the officer's bellowed commands.

If the order is successfully issued, the ordered unit immediately shoots at any visible target. If the enemy is up to 12" away, models firing lasguns fire three shots, rather than just two. If the unit did not move in its Movement phase they fire two shots with their lasguns at an enemy up to 24" away, instead of just one.

Incoming! The officer orders his men to dig in, making use of trenches and foxholes dug earlier to brace themselves against the storm of incoming fire.

If the order is successfully issued, the ordered unit immediately goes to ground. The ordered unit receives +2 to its cover save, rather than the normal bonus. Note that this means the squad will not be able to act normally until the end of the player's following turn.

Move! Move! Move! The officer exhorts his troops to sprint towards their objective, be it a strategic point or shelter from enemy fire, at the double.

If the order is successfully issued, the ordered unit immediately runs, rolling three dice and using the highest result when determining how far they move.

Wargear

Platoon Standard: Whilst the standard bearer is still alive, his squad counts as scoring an additional wound for the purposes of calculating close combat results.

INFANTRY SQUAD

Imperial Guard platoons are made up of several ten-man squads, led into battle by a low-ranking commander such as a sergeant. Infantry Squads form the backbone of the Imperial Guard. Countless billions of soldiers fight and die for the Imperium. They are the footsloggers, the dogfaces, the poor bloody infantry. Guardsmen are used for every conceivable action the Imperial Guard may undertake, from holding ground to forlorn charges against enemy positions.

The armies of the Imperial Guard are made from billions of regiments, recruited from every world in the Imperium. There is no universal uniform for Imperial Guardsmen; warriors don the armour and wargear native to their home worlds – the only piece of armament common to all Imperial Guardsmen is the lasgun, and even then some regiments have been raised with only muskets, crossbows, or even spears. The fighting ability of each regiment reflects the world and society it comes from. Some planets breed savage gang fighters whilst others raise primitive and barbaric warriors.

Imperial Guardsmen are disciplined troops indoctrinated to follow orders to the letter. In the face of the enemy the serried ranks of the Imperial Guard are trained to stand firm and respond with a steady aim. When sergeants bellow the rank and file obey; backs stiffen and lasguns level at the foe. Opponents charging at Imperial Guard positions must first survive a blazing hail of lasfire, a fusillade that can stem the tide of all but the most determined assault. The fate of battles is often decided upon the courage and mettle of Infantry Squads, however, they are still only men. On equal terms they are no match for the many alien horrors they must face. Should such enemies close the distance the Infantry Squads are, more often than not, slaughtered.

Although some Guardsmen are equipped with a variety of powerful and specialised weaponry, the primary strength of the infantry regiments remains their huge and expendable mass of manpower. The combined firepower of Imperial Guard regiments makes them a deadly opponent, capable of out-shooting almost any enemy. The thundering charge of a thousand Guardsmen can overwhelm the most elite and dangerous of opponents, crushing them underfoot and running them through with a wall of bayonet points.

Conscripts

In dire situations a world may be required to increase its tithe and raise additional regiments to match some overwhelming threat. A planet may be forced to bring forward its annual conscription, recruiting troops who would otherwise be deemed too young, or have not had the time to complete basic training. These youths are officially designated as probitors. In practice, they are given a variety of nicknames, but the most common moniker is 'Whiteshield'. This name stems from the fact that they show no regimental, company or platoon markings until they have earned the right to do so on the battlefield. The only insignia these recruits display are white helmet stripes. Eager to prove their courage, these reckless cadets enter the fray. Those few that survive might one day be lucky enough to call themselves 'Guardsmen' – far more than a simple promotion, this is a rite of passage amongst the probitors that marks their entry into adulthood.

	WS	BS	S	T	W	I	A	Ld	Sv
Guardsman	3	3	3	3	1	3	1	7	5+
Sergeant	3	3	3	3	1	3	2	8	5+
Heavy Weapons Team	3	3	3	3	2	3	2	7	5+
Conscript	2	2	3	3	1	3	1	5	5+

Special Rules

Combined Squad: Infantry Squads (not other infantry units such as Conscripts, Veterans, Heavy Weapons Squads etc.) have the option of forming Combined Squads. The decision to form Combined Squads must be made at deployment. If the Imperial Guard player wishes to deploy his forces in this way then any Infantry Squad may join another Infantry Squad from the same platoon. For example, an Infantry Platoon consisting of a Platoon Command Squad and three ten-man Infantry Squads can instead choose to deploy as a Platoon Command Squad and a single thirty-man Infantry Squad, or a Platoon Command Squad, a ten-man Infantry Squad and a twenty-man Infantry Squad. Combined Squads may not embark into vehicles that have insufficient transport capacity to carry the entire Combined Squad.

If you decide to form any squads into larger units, then they are of course treated as a single unit from that point. Combined Squads may not split up into their constituent component units again during the game.

HEAVY WEAPONS SQUAD

While the massed Infantry Squads of the Imperial Guard can overwhelm many foes by their sheer numbers, it falls to Heavy Weapons Squads to deliver the killing blow. All Imperial Guard regiments include some form of mobile heavy weapons, especially those with limited access to armoured fighting vehicles. These sections bolster the battle line and provide close fire support. Unleashing a torrent of indiscriminate firepower, a Heavy Weapons Team can reduce the packed ranks of the enemy to nothing but a pile of bleeding corpses in the time it takes to pull a trigger.

Those soldiers demonstrating an affinity with specialised weaponry are gathered together into squads within a heavy weapons company. Imperial Guard heavy weapons are crewed by a team of two troopers; generally speaking, one crewman carries and fires the weapon whilst the other hauls and loads the ammunition.

It is rare for a regiment's entire heavy weapons company to fight together and the individual teams are usually assigned to other companies as platoon-support units. Placed under the command of an officer, the Heavy Weapons Teams boost the firepower of the individual squads, allowing them to engage enemy armoured units or hold off alien hordes that outnumber them many times over. Organising these teams into dedicated Heavy Weapons Squads, typically numbering three Heavy Weapons Teams, allows that concentrated

firepower to be more easily directed. Entire columns of battle tanks can be targeted and exterminated in short order with massive salvos of firepower.

Some squads use mortars to rain high-explosive shells upon enemy positions that would otherwise be out of reach. Mortars pin down the enemy whilst other Imperial Guard units move in for the kill. Other Heavy Weapons Squads act as fire support teams and armed with heavy bolters or autocannons, they lay down a curtain of firepower that can mow down packed ranks of infantry in a welter of gore and tear apart light vehicles. When equipped with the largest man-portable weapons in the regiment, Heavy Weapons Squads are excellent anti-tank units. Such teams use lascannons and krak missiles to pick out heavy vehicles, large alien creatures and other armoured targets.

Special Weapon Squads

Most regiments maintain a separate support company dedicated to providing infantry platoons with troops armed and trained to fulfill a number of specialist roles. These six-man squads may be sniper teams, demolitions experts, combat engineers and the like. Snipers work with spotters to target enemy commanders, whilst those armed with heavy explosives perform tasks such as destroying fortifications. Combat engineers are particularly feared by the enemy and can clear out bunkers with gouts of lethal flame.

	WS	BS	S	T	W	I	A	Ld	Sv
Heavy Weapons Team	3	3	3	3	2	3	2	7	5+
Guardsman	3	3	3	3	1	3	1	7	5+

The Ubiquitous Lasgun

The lasgun is the universal small arm of the Imperial Guard, but there are a great many models, marks and patterns in service. The Cadian Shock Troops, for example, commonly bear the M36 lasrifle, originally manufactured on Kantrael, a weapon known for its robustness. The Catachan Jungle Fighters bear the Mk 4 lascarbine, which has less cowling than the M36 and is therefore lighter and easier to carry in close environs. Other common marks include the easily mass-manufactured Mars and Armageddon lasguns, the much sought after variable power setting Triplex pattern and the short-barrelled, folding-stock models used by mechanised infantry, tank crews and troops on starship detail. Even more exotic are the intricately wrought heirloom weapons of the Vostroyan Firstborn, and the Accatran pattern mark IV, much valued by the Elysians and other drop troopers for its compactness and utility at short range.

CHIMERA ARMOURED TRANSPORT

The Chimera is the Imperial Guard's most commonly used armoured troop carrier. These ubiquitous vehicles are extremely durable and practical, capable of mounting an array of support weapons. From within the armoured confines of a Chimera, an embarked Infantry Squad can utilise the hull-mounted firing points to unleash a lethal fusillade of shots into the foe, protected from all but the most destructive of reprisals.

Chimeras are a potent symbol of the might of the Imperial Guard and are fitted with a range of equipment, including searchlights to locate the enemy and massive bulldozer blades to clear a path for heavier battle tanks. With scanners and communication voxes, Chimeras are also suitable mobile bases of operations from which Imperial Guard officers can marshal their forces.

Squads of Imperial Guardsmen mounted in Chimeras are often referred to as Armoured Fist units. These squads lend speed and tactical flexibility to the often slow and rigid formations of the Imperial Guard. An infantry regiment does not typically include any mechanised troops, it being difficult for most planetary governors to obtain and maintain the vehicles needed for such formations. Because of this, it is quite common for commanders to attach individual Armoured Fist squads from fully mechanised regiments in order to provide fast-moving armoured transport.

> "Do not strike until you are ready to crush the enemy utterly, and then attack without mercy, destroy every vestige of resistance, leave no one to work against you."
>
> The Tactica Imperium

Armoured Fist squads are able to respond quickly to emergent threats or forge ahead of the main advance and seize vital objectives until ground pounding reinforcements arrive. Enemy positions are quickly overrun; the heavy weaponry of Chimeras spitting a stream of death into the packed ranks of the foe before Infantry Squads charge out of the steel ramps at the vehicles' rear and despatch survivors at point blank range. Armoured Fist squads have a reputation for 'getting the job done' and are in high demand by infantry commanders. Typically deployed against the most heavily defended of enemy positions where the armoured protection of a Chimera is vital for a successful assault, it is no surprise that Armoured Fist squads have an even higher rate of attrition than standard infantry formations.

Over the millennia, the Chimera has been pressed into service in a variety of different forms, proving its reliability and worth time and again. The Chimera is a highly versatile vehicle able to operate in the most hostile environments. Chimeras are amphibious and are able to move through dense swamps, deep marshes and even rivers. Many an enemy army has been destroyed because its general thought his flanks protected by such obstructions, only to find ranks of Imperial Guardsmen, supported by the fearsome anti-personnel weaponry of their Chimera transports, disgorging into the very heart of his forces.

	BS	Armour			Type
		F	S	R	
Chimera	3	12	10	10	Tank

Transport
A Chimera has a transport capacity of twelve models.

Fire Points: Five models can fire from the Chimera's top hatch. In reality, several are firing from the fixed lasgun emplacements along either flank, but for simplicity we assume all shots to be taken from the hatch.

Access Points: Chimeras have one access point at the rear.

Special Rules
Amphibious: A Chimera treats all water features as clear terrain when it moves.

Mobile Command Vehicle: An officer embarked within a Chimera may still issue orders to squads. Measure range and line of sight from any point of the Chimera's hull.

VETERANS

Imperial Guard regiments are often called upon to fight gruelling wars of attrition for years and even decades at a time. As time passes, each company will shrink in size as casualties take their inevitable toll. Those that survive are the hardiest troopers in the Imperial Guard. Their battlefield training has been honed in the fires of war, forging them into warriors who have learnt how to fight and kill with lethal efficiency. Veterans are the hard core of the Imperial Guard, the first squad in an assault and the last in a retreat.

Veterans are natural born survivors. They have escaped ambushes, negotiated mine fields and fought a myriad of foes and lived to tell the tale. Their continued existence, despite the dangers they face, is testament to both their skill at war and their natural survival instinct. The toughest and most skilled of the Imperial Guard's regiments may have endured throughout the grim wars of a campaign with their forces largely unscathed. These legendary regiments have a heroic reputation and have entire companies comprised of battle-proven killers. This is highly unusual however and after an especially hard campaign, often all that is left of a company is a single squad of combat-hardened Veterans who have survived where their comrades have fallen. Such squads are attached to larger regiments where it is hoped they will assimilate quickly and their skills may rub off onto less-experienced shoulders. These Veterans may not be from the same regiment or even the same home world, and so

may introduce brand new combat-tactics and an entirely different war-ethic to their foster regiment.

Although Veteran squads technically remain part of the same rigid command structure, these grizzled survivors function best when allowed a certain amount of free rein. They provide valuable battlefield experience and may employ unconventional, but effective tactics – such as the laying of booby traps – that are not taught by the Tactica Imperialis.

Veterans excel in all aspects of warfare, from close-range firefights to heavy demolitions work. Veterans are all inevitably deadeye shots and such warriors are usually kept together to bolster the line, their superior marksmanship making the difference between defeat and victory.

Many Veterans carry weapons and wargear not commonly issued to the massed ranks of the Imperial Guardsmen. An extra grenade here or a shotgun there can make the difference between life and death. Veteran squads acquire these non-standard armaments from a variety of sources. Many Veterans receive additional training in order to perform dedicated combat roles and have accordingly been issued the necessary equipment. Some are 'borrowed' from Munitorum stores, whilst others are battlefield trophies prized out of the cold, dead hands of a fallen corpse and taken as spoils of war.

	WS	BS	S	T	W	I	A	Ld	Sv
Veteran	3	4	3	3	1	3	1	7	5+
Veteran Sergeant	3	4	3	3	1	3	2	8	5+
Veteran Weapons Team	3	4	3	3	2	3	2	7	5+

Wargear

Snare Mines: Veteran squads acting as forward sentries carry snare mines to defend their firing positions. Each consists of a concussion grenade and a proximity detonator. They are capable of disorienting oncoming enemies, leaving them vulnerable to counter-attack. A squad with snare mines is counted as having defensive grenades.

> ### Combining Regiments
> With few exceptions, regiments are not reinforced with troops from their own home worlds. Instead, under-strength formations are merged to form composite regiments. Where possible, the formations joined are from the same home world, as was the case when the 12th and 78th Cadian were merged after the Fall of Ice Hive Magnox, forming the 12th/78th Cadian. Sometimes, however, two very different regiments are combined, such as when the 182nd Catachan was merged with the 90th Elysian. As this took place on the Departmento Munitorum world of Prosan, the composite regiment was designated the 314th Prosan. This particular merging proved highly successful. The new regiment became expert in airmobile jungle warfare after being issued Valkyries during the the Saikong Justification wars.

PENAL LEGION TROOPERS

The Penal Legions are made up of the scum of the galaxy. Their ranks are drawn from Imperial Guard troops who have committed capital crimes, and had their sentences commuted to life service. They are a savage band of desperate cut-throats: some half-crazed with anger, others driven mad with remorse. Reprieved from the death cells because of some talent or uncanny instinct, these dregs comprise the most vicious, ill-tempered and unstable group of psychopaths and killers in the Imperial Guard.

Discipline is by necessity harsh in the Imperial Guard where there are transgressions of military law that cannot go unpunished. While it may sometimes be prudent to turn a blind eye to a drunken brawl the same cannot be said when men turn upon and kill each other by accident or design. Such men – killers, rogues, thieves, cowards and deserters – must face the choice between death, and service in the Penal Legion. There are a great many capital crimes in the Imperium, so the supply of 'volunteers' for the Penal Legions is never-ending.

The troops sentenced to service in the Penal Legions are there for the rest of their invariably short lives. They must live under a tremendous burden of guilt; for not only have they committed crimes, but in doing so, they have also betrayed the Emperor. For those Legionnaires who are genuinely repentant, the opportunity to alleviate this burden is fully embraced and many die on the battlefield in a desperate attempt to atone for their crimes. In rare and exceptional circumstances, Legionnaires who complete their missions and survive might be granted the Emperor's pardon. These Legionnaires are absolved of their sins and can then rejoin the ranks of the Imperial Guard, and although such a thing occurs only a handful of times a millennia, it is a glimmer of hope these damned souls cling to.

New Legionnaires have their heads shaved and tattooed with their unit insignia. Explosive collars are clamped around their necks. The collars are a disciplinary device, primarily designed to discourage a prisoner from attempting to escape. The blast from one is directed inwards and will have little effect on anyone standing nearby other than showering them in a fountain of blood and gore. In battle the collars are detonated by a Penal Custodian, when discipline needs to be enforced without destroying the troopers' morale.

Whilst the Penal Legions are home to the human refuse of the Imperium, amongst them can be found some of the most skilled warriors of the Imperial Guard, reckless heroes whose specialised skills are required by the Emperor once again. Banded into covert teams, Penal Legionnaires are tasked with the most dangerous missions where their unorthodox abilities and unique skills are essential for victory. They include soldiers from many different regiments, repentant souls who have chosen to fight and redeem themselves in battle for crimes against their fellows. Some want to die in battle and forget their disgrace, but the toughest, the most dangerous, the born killers, somehow survive. For every hundred pathetic miscreants that die whimpering under the enemy guns, one mad killer emerges triumphant, screaming his insane anger.

	WS	BS	S	T	W	I	A	Ld	Sv
Penal Legionnaire	3	3	3	3	1	3	1	8	5+
Penal Custodian	3	3	3	3	1	3	2	8	5+

Special Rules
Scouts, Stubborn.

Desperadoes: Penal Legionnaires are rugged and resourceful, having survived many a dangerous situation by the skin of their teeth. Roll a D6 for each Penal Legion squad in your army before deployment, to determine each squad's specialist skill.

D6   Result

1-2   Gunslingers: Desperation lends the Legionnaires a boost of speed whenever a firefight breaks out – their lasguns are treated as being Assault 2, not Rapid Fire.

3-4   Psychopaths: In for a penny, in for a pound of flesh. The Legionnaires have the Counter-Attack, Fleet and Furious Charge special rules.

5-6   Knife Fighters: He who lives dirty, fights dirty. The Legionnaires are counted as having an extra close combat weapon in addition to their normal wargear. In addition, close combat attacks made by the Penal Legionnaires have the Rending special rule.

OGRYNS

Ogryns are abhumans – descendents of human populated worlds scattered throughout the Imperium and isolated from the rest of Mankind for millennia.

Ogryns are massive brutes whose immense strength is legendary throughout the Imperium. Ogryns' combat role tends to be as close assault troops where their bulk, determination and lack of imagination gives them a considerable advantage. They thunder into enemy troops, smashing the 'little 'uns' to a paste with broad swings of their stocky weapons. They can survive a score of wounds that would fell a normal man and shrug off small-arms fire as if it were nothing more than a bothersome sump-fly. Ogryns are dim-witted thugs who respond to any and all threats with overwhelming power and extreme violence, whether it is required or not.

Ogryns have a natural aptitude for combat and their notorious stupidity means they benefit little from training. Because of this, Ogryns are often pressed directly into service where they form units of fearsome auxiliaries. As the most natural thing for an Ogryn to do with any heavy object is to smash it over his enemy's head, their standard issue ripper guns are sturdily constructed, lest they fall apart in the melee. The trigger mechanism of a ripper gun also incorporates a burst limiter to prevent the firer shooting off the entire drum at once – an extremely entertaining possibility that would appeal to Ogryns but swiftly leave them without ammunition.

Once befriended Ogryns are completely loyal, indeed, so eager are they to please their masters that they will happily undergo any hardship to fulfill their orders, so long as they can remember what they were. Ogryns have the same values of personal loyalty, physical toughness and determination that are common amongst many of the more barbaric cultures in the Imperium and such groups tend to get on famously well.

A select few Ogryns, those that show a glimmer of initiative or intelligence, become prime candidates for augmetic cranial surgery to boost their brain-power to the point where they can understand basic strategy and tactics, equivalent to that of an eight-year-old human child. Those that survive the biochemical Ogryn neural enhancement procedure are referred to as 'Bone 'eads', and they lead their abhuman kin in battle with considerable pride.

Ogryns hate dark confined spaces and often have to be tricked or else 'convinced' to embark into armoured transport carriers such as Chimeras. Cunning Imperial Guard officers have learnt to lure the Ogryns into transport vehicles with the assistance of a friendly faced trooper with a barrel of rations. Once the Ogryns are onboard, the vehicle's ramp is shut tight behind them. It is a thankless task for the poor Imperial Guardsman who inevitably gets stuck in the cramped confines of the vehicle's hold with the foul-smelling, bulky abhumans, who have scant regard for personal hygiene and are prone to violent, unrelenting bouts of motion sickness.

	WS	BS	S	T	W	I	A	Ld	Sv
Ogryn	4	3	5	5	3	2	3	6	5+
Ogryn Bone 'ead	4	3	5	5	3	2	4	7	5+

"A small mind is easily filled with faith."

Commissar Exen Treuer, 23rd Moradia

Special Rules
Furious Charge, Stubborn.

Bulky: Ogryns are colossal thugs with thick-set frames and immense guts. Each Ogryn counts as two models for the purposes of transport capacity.

Wargear
Ripper Gun: The ripper gun is an enormous, drum-fed automatic combat shotgun developed for the exclusive use of Ogryn units. At short range the hail of low velocity shot produced by ripper guns is so dense that it is all but impossible for the Ogryns to miss.

Range	Strength	AP	Type
12"	5	-	Assault 3

RATLINGS

Ratlings are a breed of human-descended abhumans who are characteristically short and rotund. These qualities do not make for good warriors, and they are unsuited for many battlefield roles, but none the less Ratling home worlds contribute troops to the Imperial Guard. Ratlings have a few considerable talents that make them invaluable to the Imperium; they have incredible eyesight and their small size enables them to move stealthily in close terrain which larger troops might have difficulty negotiating. These traits mean they are ideally suited to the role of snipers, and it is in this capacity that they are recruited into the Imperial Guard.

Ratlings are famously good shots, even without the telescopic laser-sights of their needle-rifles. With careful, methodical aim the Ratlings place their crosshairs, targeting the vulnerable eyes of alien beasts or the exposed joints of armoured foes. They snipe enemy commanders and tank crews with contemptuous ease, amused at the panic and confusion they wreak. In battle, Ratlings excel at infiltrating the warzone unseen, secreting themselves wherever there is cover, whether it be amongst the undergrowth of a forest world, the craters of a bomb-scarred tundra or within the twisted remnants of a ruined building. Any position that has a commanding field of fire will do, and one which reduces the possibility of any actual physical combat is even better.

Like other abhuman regiments, Ratlings have a very specific area of competence and it is quite usual to divide these teams of skilled sharpshooters into smaller units that are then placed under the command of other regimental officers. Ratlings are often the butt of soldier's jokes; however, more than one unit of Guardsmen has had cause to be grateful for the covering fire from a unit of these stout snipers.

As well as making excellent marksmen, Ratlings have a well-deserved reputation for being brilliant cooks. In many units they perform both functions, acting as the company's marksmen on the battlefield and running the kitchen at other times. The Ratling's love of food is well known and the sneaky little abhumans have a knack of 'acquiring' extra supplies to supplement their diet. Despite their diminutive size they tend to eat almost twice the ration allowance of a regular trooper. It is not unknown for some more unscrupulous Ratling entrepreneurs to offer their foster regiment a share in these spoils, the mess halls acting as a convincing front to throw off the suspicions of any mistrusting Commissars. Anything from common lho sticks to the general's finest amasec can be obtained, even prohibited narcotics such as obscura, if you're willing to pay. The Ratlings do not limit their black-marketeering to food stores alone and much of the non-standard issue weaponry common amongst the more veteran troopers has been obtained courtesy of 'the chef's special'.

In 742.M41 the Imperium launched the Damocles Gulf Crusade against the newly discovered Tau Empire. Many battle-honours were won during the short but intense conflict, but one victory in particular stands out, for it was due to a single shot fired by a lowly Ratling sniper.

It was during the advance on Gal'bryn city, the capital of the Sept World of Dal'yth, that the Ratling sniper Magogg made the shot of his life. Magogg and his squad were foraging ahead of the army when they spotted a column of Tau grav-tanks moving cautiously towards the Imperium's flank. To the Ratlings' amazement, the column halted, only 300 metres from their position. Hefting his trusty rifle and squinting down its telescopic site, Magogg calmly surveyed the aliens as they dismounted and gathered in conversation with one of their number dressed in long, flowing robes. Magogg guessed that this individual was some sort of leader, and settled his crosshair right between the alien's eyes. He took the shot, blew the alien's head clean off, and in an instant the entire Tau column was in disarray.

The Imperium's flank was saved. Magogg had achieved the first recorded kill against one of the enigmatic Tau Ethereals, and the Imperium had learnt a valuable lesson in combating this new foe.

	WS	BS	S	T	W	I	A	Ld	Sv
Ratling	2	4	2	2	1	4	1	6	5+

Special Rules
Infiltrate, Stealth.

ROUGH RIDERS

On worlds where it is usual for warriors to fight from horseback, the Imperium recruits regiments of Rough Riders. On these planets, fierce nomadic clans and warrior horse-lodges have perfected the art of cavalry techniques through years of bloodshed. Rough Riders retain many ferocious customs of their home worlds such as ritual scarring and tribal tattoos. The steeds are as tough and dangerous (and often ill-tempered) as the warriors who ride them. Such mounts are bred for power and strength, and many are given bio-chem treatments to enhance their combat potential. Trained for a life of battle, these warhorses do not shy away from the enemy or panic easily.

Whilst the majority of Rough Riders are raised from feral, undeveloped worlds this is not exclusively the case. On some planets the honour of riding a steed to war is reserved for the elite classes, formalised horse-warrior aristocracies that have accumulated generations of cavalry experience.

Even the Imperial Guard, with its legions of machinery and fighting vehicles, has a place for these fierce mounted warriors. Regiments of Rough Riders are sometimes deployed wholesale, especially where terrain is unsuitable for the tracked vehicles of the Imperial Guard. A squad of skilled cavalry can be an effective assault and skirmishing force, able to move rapidly over the broken ground, climb steep slopes and gallop along narrow ravines. However, it is more

common to divide mounted regiments and allocate Rough Rider squads to fight alongside conventional infantry regiments where they act as scouts, patrols, and fast response troops. Rough Riders are used to operating out on their own beyond the normal lines of communication, often deep inside enemy territory. Able to forage and subsist off the land, Rough Riders are able to function for extended durations behind enemy lines with only the minimum of basic supplies. Because they employ living mounts rather than machines they need neither fuel nor maintenance and, unlike vehicles, they cannot be easily traced with auspex or scanner. As such they are often utilised to harass enemy troop movements by means of hit-and-run tactics.

The mobility and speed of Rough Riders makes them a potent force on the battlefield, able to spearhead an attack as easily as running a flanking manoeuvre. Rough Riders carry a variety of weapons but the most deadly is, without doubt, the explosive-tipped hunting lance derived from the lethal spear heads used by cavalry on their home worlds to hunt down large carnivorous animals. When they confront the enemy, Rough Riders charge into the opposing lines with their explosive weapons, changing to lasgun and pistol after the initial onslaught. The thundering momentum of a cavalry charge as it crashes into the ranks of the enemy leaves only death and carnage in its wake. Those foes not impaled are pulped beneath the heavy hooves of powerful steeds.

	WS	BS	S	T	W	I	A	Ld	Sv
Rough Rider	3	3	3	3	1	3	1	7	5+
Rough Rider Sergeant	3	3	3	3	1	3	2	8	5+

Wargear

Hunting Lance: Rough Riders are armed with a long hunting lance tipped with a shaped explosive charge that can tear through even the toughest armour.

Rough Riders use their hunting lances the first time they charge into close combat, after which they cannot be used again. When they charge into close combat, a unit armed with hunting lances counts as being armed with power weapons that strike at Strength and Initiative 5. Models using a hunting lance cannot gain an extra attack from having an additional close combat weapon.

"I have seen war in all its forms. I have seen feral world savages braining each other with stones, and I have monitored the death of a whole planet at the hands of a virus bomb. I have seen Space Marines drop to certain death, and win. I have seen Titans crush whole platoons underfoot.

But there is no more stirring sight in war than the charge of massed cavalry."

Dravin Gratz, 14th Tharinga

SENTINELS

The Sentinel is a one-man all-terrain bipedal vehicle, used by the Imperial Guard where mobile patrols must be mounted across rough terrain, or where firepower must be deployed rapidly in response to a threat. Sentinels are robust vehicles, able to negotiate terrain that would immobilise heavier battle tanks and armoured vehicles.

Employed primarily for reconnaissance and light infantry support, the Sentinel Scout Walker is used by many Imperial Guard regiments to locate and obliterate knots of enemy resistance in daring ambushes and surprise attacks. Bursts from multi-lasers and gouts of super-heated promethium eliminate swathes of enemy troops. Sentinel Scout Walkers are fitted with sophisticated gyro-stabilisers to assist them as they traverse the rockiest cratered battlefield and the steepest of slopes. Articulated legs enable Sentinels to stalk quietly through dense undergrowth or urban ruins whilst permitting an impressive burst of speed over open territory. The scout vehicles' powerplants also incorporate noise-reduction modification so as not to alert the enemy to their presence. The crewmen of these Sentinels often adapt their vehicles further and all manner of rough terrain innovations are seen, from giant chainsaws to clear a path through thick jungles to servo-driven claw spikes that grip to glacial planes.

The Sentinel Scout Walker is not intended for extended frontline combat operations. The crew compartment that allows the pilot to survey his prey leaves him vulnerable to small-arms fire and the walker itself lacks the ablative armour and ferro-steel plating of a fully-fledged battle tank.

Sentinels become superb frontline units when they are modified with extra armour, able to stride through a deluge of weapons fire that would cripple or destroy a lighter insurgency walker. The mechanical legs of an Armoured Sentinel are modified with recoil compensators in place of additional gyro-stabilisers to allow the walkers to fire the most powerful of weapon systems. Sensor arrays and auspex systems are replaced with additional power cells and cooling systems to allow the Armoured Sentinel to fulfill its role as a mobile heavy weapons platform. Armoured Sentinels are used as roving hunter-killer units, search and destroy teams that stalk enemy battle tanks and eliminate them with practised efficiency, plasma and lascannon fire slicing through the thickest ablative plating. Armoured Sentinels march beside the regiments of the Imperial Guard laying waste to the foe without breaking stride.

Sentinels are often deployed far from Imperium supply lines, deep within enemy territory. When operating as autonomous units, the pilots of Sentinel squadrons are often forced to use their own initiative – a quality that is not generally fostered in Imperial soldiers. As a result, many Sentinel pilots have acquired a reputation as insubordinate hotshot mavericks.

	WS	BS	S	F	S	R	I	A
				Armour				
Scout Sentinel (Walker, Open-topped)	3	3	5	10	10	10	3	1
Armoured Sentinel (Walker)	3	3	5	12	10	10	3	1

Special Rules
Scout (Scout Sentinel only),
Move Through Cover (Scout Sentinel only).

"Always endeavour to fight the enemy on your own terms. If you outnumber the foe use reserves to break through when the enemy's overstretched lines collapse. If you are outnumbered then concentrate your forces so that the enemy can fight only your best troops. If you are powerful at close quarters then engage in dense terrain where your advantage will prove greatest. If you are superior at long range then attack along an extended front. Remember always, however, that a commander who puts his faith in heavy weaponry alone will be easily outmanoeuvred and a commander who relies on close combat without adequate support will lose his force to disciplined fire. No one has ever won a battle who failed to take advantage of his enemy's weakness, or take heed of his own."

Lord Solar Macharius,
prior to the conquest of Kallastin.

STORM TROOPERS

Storm Troopers are recruited from the orphan sons of Imperial officials – such as planetary governors or high ranking members of the Imperial Guard or Navy – from all over the galaxy. These privileged young orphans are raised by the Schola Progenium. Here they are schooled to love the Emperor and are shown the many ways in which they can earn his gratitude and repay their debt to the Imperium for their upbringing. They gladly embrace a demanding and unremitting regime of prayer, study and physical exercise. Years of punishing training have honed the minds, bodies and skills of the Storm Troopers to the very peak of human perfection. Storm Troopers form the Imperial Guard's best fighting force. They are ruthless, proficient killers whose combat skills within the Imperial Guard are second to none.

To complement their superior training, Storm Troopers are better armed and armoured than regular Guardsmen. Protected by rigid arma-plas and reinforced ceramite plates, Storm Troopers can wade through a torrent of small-arms fire that would kill a normal Guardsmen outright. The sophisticated hot-shot laser weapons wielded by Storm Troopers are more potent and destructive than the standard lasgun. The increased power from such a weapon is ideally suited to the Storm Troopers' shock assault role. However, such weapons require reinforced barrels, thermal-cooling cells and gyro-stabilised power packs, all of which makes them difficult to produce and maintain. The Departmento

Munitorum rarely issues these weapons to soldiers outside of Storm Trooper companies, who are trained to look after and even rebuild the weapons if necessary.

Storm Troopers are constantly moving from one war zone to another and are amongst the most experienced units in the Imperial Guard. It is rare that the entirety of the Storm Trooper regiment will fight in one place. Instead, individual companies are sent to bolster the strength of the Imperial Guard present, providing a core of ultra-trained squads that can be deployed as needed. The special treatment and elite status given to Storm Troopers causes a certain amount of rancour amongst regular troops who refer to them as 'Glory Boys' or 'Big Toy Soldiers', but none who witness their skill at arms can deny that they are worthy of such standing.

Storm Troopers are taught to perform covert operations, spearhead assaults into fortified positions and storm key installations. They can deploy ahead of the rest of an army, infiltrating behind enemy lines to engage the foe and cause maximum confusion. They are often dropped into the midst of the enemy during battle. Leaping from low-flying aircraft and descending using grav-chutes, Storm Troopers land into the middle of fierce firefights, guns blazing before they even hit the ground. Storm Troopers sweep through resistance with the force of a tornado, controlled bursts of precision lasfire leaving a trail of twitching corpses in their wake.

	WS	BS	S	T	W	I	A	Ld	Sv
Storm Trooper	3	4	3	3	1	3	1	7	4+
Storm Trooper Sergeant	3	4	3	3	1	3	2	8	4+

Special Rules
Deep Strike.

Special Operations. Storm Troopers are not lightly cast into battle – they are always given a specific mission to achieve, too important to be entrusted to others. Before deployment, declare to your opponent which mission each Storm Trooper squad in your army is following.

> **Reconnaissance:** The reconnaissance mission grants the Scouts and Move Through Cover special rules.

> **Airborne Assault:** The airborne assault mission allows the Storm Trooper squad to re-roll the scatter dice when they Deep Strike.

> **Behind Enemy Lines:** The behind enemy lines mission grants the squad the Infiltrate special rule and their weapons count as Pinning the first time the squad fires.

Wargear
Hot-shot Lasgun: The hot-shot lasgun uses a more powerful, external energy cell. This allows the hellgun to project a much more powerful, and more penetrating, shot.

Range	Strength	AP	Type
18"	3	3	Rapid Fire

PSYKER BATTLE SQUAD

Psyker Battle Squads are teams of Sanctioned Psykers who have yet to complete their psychic training. Accompanied by ever-vigilant Overseers – strong-willed individuals who act as wardens, minders, protectors and, if necessary, merciful executioners – the Sanctioned Psykers are guided towards the enemy where they use their collective powers to create maelstroms of woe and destruction.

During their training at the Scholastica Psykana, psykers are taught to use their innate gifts. It takes decades of tutelage and practice before they learn to grasp a fraction of their limited powers. Many are not yet prepared to draw upon the power of the Warp unaided by more experienced psykers. Some never progress to the ranks of primary psyker, growing reclusive and disturbed by the horrors they have witnessed in their years of Warp-fuelled nightmares.

Individually these psykers are barely able to control the power they wield and are as much of a danger to their allies and themselves as they are to the enemy. Such psykers are grouped with others of their kind, for together they are able to maintain some semblance of focus. The Sanctioned Psykers that form a Psyker Battle Squad become so closely attuned to each other that they cease acting independently and instead function as a single combined consciousness. Whilst one psyker may start a sentence another shall finish it, several members of the unit chorusing and echoing the words in eerie unison. In battle they pool their energies, each member adding his psychic ability to unleash a power greater than the sum of its parts. The build-up of psychic energy is likened to the sound of a choir; where the voice of a single psyker may go unheard, together the combined might of a Psyker Battle Squad can flatten a battle tank.

In battle, the sonorous chanting of the psykers continuously rises as they draw ever deeper upon the power of the Warp. A massive surge of psychic energy breaks over into the physical world with terrible effects. Psychic thunderstorms engulf the psykers' foes, a hurricane of coruscating Warp energy that ruptures organs and tears bodies apart.

	WS	BS	S	T	W	I	A	Ld	Sv
Sanctioned Psyker	2	3	2	3	1	3	1	9	5+
Overseer	3	3	3	3	1	3	2	9	5+

Special Rules
Psyker (Sanctioned Psykers only).

Psychic Choir: The Psyker Battle Squad is treated as a single psyker for the purposes of using a psychic power. The controlling player may measure range and line of sight from any Sanctioned Psyker model when resolving psychic powers.

Ultimate Sanction: If a Psyker Battle Squad unit suffers a Perils of the Warp attack, the ever-vigilant Overseer will immediately 'save' the affected Psykers' souls. Remove D3 Sanctioned Psykers as casualties instead of resolving the attack. If the Overseer has been killed, every Sanctioned Psyker in the squad suffers a Perils of the Warp attack.

Psychic Powers
Soulstorm: The psykers engulf their enemies in a storm of Warp energy that sears flesh and rends their foes' souls from their bodies.

This is a psychic shooting attack with the following profile:

Range	Strength	AP	Type
36"	*	D6	Assault 1, Large Blast

*The Strength of the Soulstorm is equal to the number of Sanctioned Psykers in the unit utilising the power. The AP of the attack is determined randomly each time it is used.

Weaken Resolve: The psykers reach out with their minds, evoking irrational terror in the minds of their foes.

This power is used during the Psyker Battle Squad's Shooting phase. Choose one enemy unit within 36" and line of sight of the Psyker Battle Squad. For the remainder of the turn, the enemy unit's Leadership is reduced by the number of Sanctioned Psykers in the unit utilising the power (to a minimum of 2).

LEMAN RUSS BATTLE TANK

The Leman Russ is the core battle tank of the Imperial Guard and the mainstay of its armoured fighting force. It forms the spearhead of any Imperial Guard armoured attack. Armed with mighty battle cannons and heavy weapons, these lumbering brutes grind forward unleashing an indefatigable onslaught of firepower. Those enemies that do not fall to the cannonade are crushed beneath their heavy treads.

Most of the Leman Russ Battle Tanks fighting as part of an infantry company are detached from an 'Emperor's Fist' or 'Emperor's Lance' armoured regiment. It is rare indeed for an Imperial Guard force to engage the enemy without at least one of these fearsome machines in support.

The Imperial Guard has used the rugged and easily maintained design of the Leman Russ for millennia. It is by no means the most sophisticated vehicle in the Imperium, however, its adaptability and ability to keep on working no matter what an inexperienced crew may do to it has made it arguably the most successful battle tank in the galaxy. Its sturdy and efficient engines will run on virtually any fuel and will keep the armoured tank trudging forward despite all but the most hostile of environments.

The Leman Russ is a slow, ponderous beast in comparison to some vehicles in the Imperial Guard. However, no other tank of its size comes close to matching the sheer weight of firepower these armoured powerhouses can unleash or withstand. The armour casing of a Leman Russ is designed to be tough, long-lasting and easy to repair. The reinforced hull and ferro-steel plating of a Leman Russ is proof against all but the most destructive of enemy attacks and can sustain a deluge of damage before yielding. Small-arms fire patters harmlessly from its armoured form as it drives onwards heedless of incoming shells and energy blasts.

Inside the Leman Russ's armoured shell it is hot, cramped and so noisy that it is all but impossible to hear anything over the rumble of engines and the din of weapons fire. It requires a minimum of four crew to operate a Leman Russ battle tank, with another two added to this number if side sponsons are fitted. Although they are not universally included, these sponsons are integral to the design of the Leman Russ and can be fitted with a variety of deadly weapons. A dedicated gunner mans each and, together with the primary turret, they supply a torrent of fire that hammers the enemy into oblivion.

Special Rules

Lumbering Behemoth. A Leman Russ that moved at combat speed or remained stationary can fire its turret weapon in addition to any other weapons it is usually allowed to fire (even if the turret weapon is ordnance!). However, a Leman Russ travelling at cruising speed can only move up to D6 + 6" – roll every time it moves at this speed.

	BS	Armour			Type
		F	S	R	
Leman Russ Battle Tank	3	14	13	10	Tank
Leman Russ Exterminator	3	14	13	10	Tank
Leman Russ Vanquisher	3	14	13	10	Tank
Leman Russ Eradicator	3	14	13	10	Tank
Leman Russ Demolisher	3	14	13	11	Tank
Leman Russ Punisher	3	14	13	11	Tank
Leman Russ Executioner	3	14	13	11	Tank

Leman Russ Battle Tank

The Leman Russ is the most common battle tank in the Imperial Guard. Its tried and tested design has stood the trials of time better than most; making it the tank most often requested by Imperial Guard officers to be attached to their infantry formations.

Battle Cannon: The battle cannon is the most common armament of the Leman Russ. The explosive rounds of a battle cannon decimate enemy infantry and tanks with equal contempt.

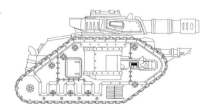

Range	Strength	AP	Type
72"	8	3	Ordnance 1, Large Blast

Leman Russ Exterminator

The Leman Russ Exterminator is a common variant of the standard design, capable of laying down a withering hail of fire against which no infantry can survive. The exterminator autocannon's rapid firing shells can tear through lightly armoured chassis as easily as they rip though flesh and bone.

Exterminator Autocannon: Utilised on the Leman Russ Exterminator, the twin barrels of an exterminator autocannon fire synchronised bursts of heavy-calibre, high velocity shells.

Range	Strength	AP	Type
48"	7	4	Heavy 4, Twin-linked

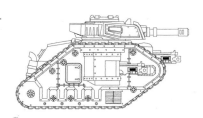

Leman Russ Vanquisher

The Leman Russ Vanquisher is becoming increasingly rare as the skills and technology required for the construction of the Vanquisher-pattern battle cannon were lost when the forge world of Tigrus was overrun. The Vanquisher cannon's long range and high first-hit kill ratio make it the anti-tank weapon of choice for most commanders.

Vanquisher Battle Cannon: The Vanquisher mounts a modified cannon that fires special anti-armour shells.

Range	Strength	AP	Type
72"	8	2	Heavy 1*

*Shots from a Vanquisher battle cannon roll an additional D6 when rolling for armour penetration.

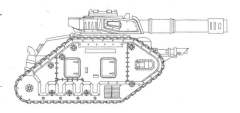

Leman Russ Eradicator

The Leman Russ Eradicator was instrumental during the urban conflict on Khai-Zhan. The blasts from its heavy, high-calibre shells can flatten both enemy barricades and any infantry sheltering behind. The tank's design is easily replicated on dozens of forge worlds and the Eradicator is utilised throughout the Imperium to support infantry fighting in dense terrain.

Eradicator Nova Cannon: Eradicator nova cannons fire shells with an unstable sub-atomic charge at their core.

Range	Strength	AP	Type
36"	6	4	Heavy 1, Large Blast*

*Cover saves may not be taken against wounds caused by an Eradicator nova cannon.

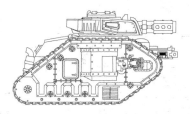

Leman Russ Demolisher

The Leman Russ Demolisher was devised for but one task: line breaking. It carries the short-ranged but highly destructive demolisher cannon. Often thought of as a siege tank, the Leman Russ Demolisher has additional armour plating and is utterly devastating when fighting against enemy fortifications.

Demolisher Siege Cannon: Short ranged but utterly lethal, no armour is proof against the might of a Demolisher siege cannon.

Range	Strength	AP	Type
24"	10	2	Ordnance 1, Large Blast

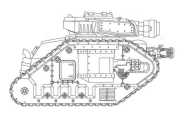

Leman Russ Punisher

The Leman Russ Punisher eschews anti-tank effectiveness for increased anti-infantry firepower. There are few other tanks in the entire Imperial Guard capable of pouring as much ammunition into the foe as a Leman Russ Punisher. The tanks' crews have reputations for being both trigger-happy and gung-ho.

Punisher Gatling Cannon: A recent addition to the Imperial Guard armoury, the Punisher gatling cannon unleashes a torrent of anti-infantry firepower.

Range	Strength	AP	Type
24"	5	–	Heavy 20

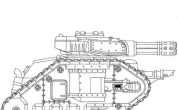

Leman Russ Executioner

The Executioner is one of the oldest variants of the Leman Russ; archives show that during the Great Crusade entire regiments of this tank were fielded. Gradually, over many millennia, understanding of plasma technology has been lost and the Executioner is now a rare technological relic.

Executioner Plasma Cannon: The Executioner plasma cannon fires pulsed plasma bursts that can incinerate even the most heavily armoured infantry.

Range	Strength	AP	Type
36"	7	2	Heavy 3, Blast

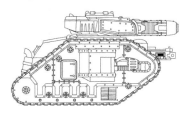

HELLHOUND FLAME TANK

The Hellhound Flame Tank is designed to flush out enemy infantry from dense terrain. A Hellhound is equipped with a powerful flamethrower that discharges a self-igniting chemical. The flames find their way into every nook and crevice, consuming any troops who are sheltering behind cover, reducing them to cinder and ash.

Only a select few volunteer to serve as part of a Hellhound crew, and these are not always the most stable of individuals. Hellhound crews have a cavalier attitude and take a perverse pride in this reputation, claiming other Guardsmen 'just can't take the heat'. In battle they gun their vehicles towards the largest concentration of enemy troops, incinerating their foes with pyromaniacal zeal.

Based upon a Chimera chassis, the Hellhound has an increased engine size in place of a troop-carrying capacity. The vast promethium tanks have also necessitated thicker armour plating. The versatility of the Hellhound design has led to several redesigns which have become increasingly common amongst Imperial Guard regiments.

		Armour			Type
	BS	F	S	R	
Hellhound	3	12	12	10	Fast, Tank
Devil Dog	3	12	12	10	Fast, Tank
Bane Wolf	3	12	12	10	Fast, Tank

Hellhound

The Hellhound has a vicious reputation, and the sight of just one of these monstrous war engines incinerating swathes of infantry with its horrifying inferno cannon, instilling fear into the hearts of the enemy. Enemy infantry flee for their lives as the dying screams and smoking remains of their comrades fill the air.

Inferno Cannon: The inferno cannon fires a lethal gout of white-hot flame over a considerable distance.

Range	Strength	AP	Type
Template*	6	4	Heavy 1

*To fire the inferno cannon place the template so that the narrow end is within 12" of the weapon and the large end is no closer to the weapon than the narrow end. The inferno cannon is then treated like any other template weapon.

Devil Dog

Devil Dogs are a variant of the more widespread Hellhound. Armed with powerful melta cannons, Devil Dogs are able to tear through heavy troops and armoured tanks in short order. When fired, the main weapons make a high-pitched howl as moisture in the air vapourises, becoming a roaring blast as the target detonates.

Melta Cannon: The melta cannon fires a thermal blast over a short distance, causing massive molecular breakdown and turning the target into a mixture of molten slag and steaming gas.

Range	Strength	AP	Type
24"	8	1	Heavy 1, Melta, Blast

Bane Wolf

Bane Wolves are used when the complete eradication of the enemy is warranted. They smother their targets in broiling clouds of noxious gas that dissolves organic material in moments. Victims' blood boils in their own veins and their flesh sloughs from bone as the mixture of toxins do their horrific work.

Chem Cannon: The chem cannon belches toxic clouds of acidic poison gas.

Range	Strength	AP	Type
Template	1	3	Heavy 1, Poisoned (2+)*

*Against targets with a Toughness value, hits from a chem cannon will always wound on a roll of 2+.

HYDRA FLAK TANK

The Hydra Flak Tank is the Imperial Guard's primary ground-based mobile weapons system for combating enemy aircraft. Once the Hydra's target is locked in its sights the evasive manoeuvres of even the most skilled enemy pilot are futile; none can escape the fusillade of the flak tank. The huge ammunition reserves and auto-loaders means the Hydra's rapid-firing weapons can chatter a near constant hail of death at its enemies, filling the skies with a seething curtain of high velocity explosive rounds that rip through lightly armoured fuselages and send aircraft plummeting towards the ground. Linked to a predictive logic-spirit, the Hydra's distinctive array of four autocannons can track the swiftest of targets. It is these enemies that fear the wrath of the Hydra the most, having eschewed heavy armour plates and relying instead upon their incredible speed and manoeuvrability for protection.

Hydra Flak Tanks are employed when air-superiority is in the balance or the Imperial Navy is unable to commit its own forces to intercept enemy aircraft. Hydra Flak Tanks are therefore an essential part of the Imperial Guard's arsenal, providing much needed anti-aircraft firepower.

Manufactured on hundreds of forge worlds, the Hydra is a common sight in the Imperial Guard, frequently deployed in support of armoured tank columns, fixed artillery emplacements and infantry regiments who would otherwise be at threat from enemy bomber strikes and strafing runs. The ponderous bulk of the Imperial Guard is particularly vulnerable to such attacks, lacking the ability to effectively evade aerial hunters.

When the threat of attack from the air is not immediate, Hydra crews have been known to put the quad-autocannons to good use against enemy infantry formations and light vehicles; the explosive rounds shredding such opponents just as effectively. The sheer weight of firepower unleashed by a Hydra can decimate entire formations in a heartbeat. Enemy infantry fall before the Hydra's guns like wheat to a scythe.

The fearsome rate of fire that a Hydra can unleash rivals that of a fully armed battle tank. When a swarm of enemy jetbikes streaks towards the Imperial frontline, it is the Hydra that can single-handedly turn the tide; a deluge of heavy caliber shells punching through the lightly armoured frames with contemptuous ease. Many an enemy grav-tank has been brought low from the Hydra's relentless firepower. Whilst they may sweep over the battlefield dodging incoming small-arms fire they meet their doom when facing a Hydra. A fiery burst from quad-autocannons sends a trail of death towards the craft, smashing through engine turbines and transforming the skimmer from a sleek blur to a blazing wreck in the blink of an eye.

	BS	Armour			Type
		F	S	R	
Hydra	3	12	10	10	Tank

Wargear

Hydra Autocannon: Designed for swatting enemy aircraft from the sky, the Hydra is death incarnate to skimmers.

Range	Strength	AP	Type
72"	7	4	Heavy 2

Auto-targeting System: Skimmers cannot claim the cover save gained due to moving flat out against shots fired by the Hydra. Similarly, bikes cannot claim the cover save gained due to turbo-boosting against shots fired by the Hydra.

Hydra Flak Tanks normally serve in batteries as part of an infantry regiment's headquarters company, or as part of the command squadron of an armoured company. But there are some regiments that consist entirely of Hydras, and these are often referred to as 'heavy air defence regiments'. Such units often find their constituent elements detached for duty across a warzone, guarding important installations from enemy air attack. Occasionally, however, a heavy air defence regiment will fight as a single formation, as was the case during the Defence of Bastion 312 when the 2nd Brimlock 'Sky Wardens' contested the rebel drop, achieving an unprecedented confirmed kill ratio of 99,999–1.

ORDNANCE BATTERY

When the Imperial Guard marches to war it is accompanied by the thunderous bombardment of artillery fire. Dedicated artillery companies comprising dozens of Ordnance Batteries fire ceaseless barrages from long range, pounding the enemy prior to a general advance. Before the smoke has cleared the infantry emerge, launching their assaults in the wake of the destructive artillery salvoes whilst the enemy is still reeling from the blows.

Of all the Imperial Guard's ordnance units, the Basilisk is the most numerous and well known. Like many of the Imperial Guard's self-propelled artillery pieces, Basilisks are fully mobile and can keep pace with infantry advances, ready to deploy for battle in a relatively short space of time. Such devastating weapons are hardly the replacement of battle tanks, their lack of ablative amour and exposed crew carriages makes them too vulnerable to lead assaults. Instead, Basilisks are, much like other artillery pieces, fielded in a support role to frontline regiments.

Basilisks can be redirected, reloaded and fired relatively swiftly and the design of the earthshaker cannon allows the weapon to be elevated to a steep enough angle for it to fire its shells high over the battlefield and onto concealed enemy targets. Although the accuracy of the earthshaker cannon is impaired when firing in this manner, it allows the Basilisk to deploy out of harm's way where the enemy is powerless to

retaliate. The powerful shells fired by a Basilisk are capable of smashing apart both infantry and vehicles with ease and the unmistakable shriek of its incoming ordnance is rightly feared by the enemies of the Emperor.

Many a lengthy siege has been brought to an abrupt conclusion by Imperial Guard artillery regiments, heavy shells breaching walls and flattening fortifications. The Imperial Guard is well equipped to deal with siege warfare and there are few bulwarks strong enough to withstand the magnitude of firepower unleashed by the Imperium's biggest guns.

At the defence of Bellephon, the disciplined gun-crews of the 388th Cadian Artillery 'Gate Wardens' destroyed the Chaos Imperator Titan *Tyraxoss*. The monstrous behemoth was smashed asunder several miles from Imperial lines in a relentless barrage from the artillery regiment's guns that lased an entire day.

		Armour			
	BS	F	S	R	Type
Basilisk	3	12	10	10	Open-topped, Tank
Medusa	3	12	10	10	Open-topped, Tank
Colossus	3	12	10	10	Open-topped, Tank
Griffon	3	12	10	10	Open-topped, Tank

"Infantry win firefights.
Tanks win battles.
Artillery win wars."

Old saying amongst Imperial Guard artillery officers

Special Rules
Accurate Bombardment (Griffons only): The Griffon's lighter payload affords greater accuracy than that of the larger calibre field guns.

When a Griffon fires its heavy mortar, the controlling player can re-roll the scatter dice if he wishes.

Wargear
Enclosed crew compartment: Some artillery vehicles, particularly those from worlds with toxic and corrosive atmospheres, are fitted with additional armour plating to protect the exposed crew carriage.

Vehicles equipped with the Enclosed Crew Compartment upgrade no longer count as being open-topped.

Basilisk

The Basilisk is a mobile artillery platform armed with a massive earthshaker cannon – a long-barrelled, breach-loaded gun with such a tremendous recoil that when fired, the very ground trembles. A Basilisk is most effective when deployed as part of a battery of siege guns, but each can also be utilised as a direct fire gun, engaging targets at short range with devastating results.

Earthshaker Cannon: Earthshaker cannons are huge, long-range artillery guns that fire massive shells fully capable of reducing a reinforced ferro-crete building to naught but rubble.

Range	Strength	AP	Type
36"-240"	9	3	Ordnance Barrage 1, Large Blast

Medusa

Unlike many of the Imperial Guards artillery pieces that fling shells high over a curtain wall, the Medusa tends to fire its heavy shells directly at, and eventually through, enemy fortifications. What a Medusa siege gun lacks in reach it more than makes up for in sheer destructive power. When tasked with breaching reinforced enemy bulwarks and heavily armoured installations a Medusa may be equipped with specialised bastion-breacher shells. These munitions sacrifice explosive yield for extra propellant and a much greater penetrative power. Armed so, a Medusa siege gun can level a bunker with only a single shot, and it is a foolish foe indeed that lingers for long in the face of such firepower.

Medusa Siege Cannon: The siege cannon fires shells designed for cracking enemy defences.

Range	Strength	AP	Type
36"	10	2	Ordnance 1, Large Blast

Bastion-breacher Shells: A Medusa armed with bastion-breacher shells always fires using the following profile:

Range	Strength	AP	Type
48"	10	1	Heavy 1, Blast*

*Shots from a bastion-breacher shell roll an additional D6 when determining armour penetration.

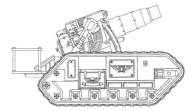

Colossus

The Colossus is one of the Imperium's most ancient and renowned artillery pieces. They are rarely seen except during campaigns where their enormous siege cannons are required to flatten enemy positions. A Colossus carries one of the largest mortars used in the Imperial Guard. Most Colossus shells are high explosive concussion munitions, which result in enormous detonation shockwaves that crush bones, crack rocks and reduce flesh to a pulp. In its delivery of ordnance, a Colossus is brutally uncompromising.

Colossus Siege Mortar: The high explosive shells fired by a Colossus siege mortar are specifically designed for crushing defenders with the rubble and ruined remains of their own defences.

Range	Strength	AP	Type
24"-240"	6	3	Ordnance Barrage 1, Large Blast*

*A Colossus siege mortar cannot fire directly. In addition, cover saves may not be taken against hits from a Colossus siege mortar.

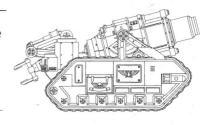

Griffon

The Griffon armoured weapon carrier is one of the most frequently employed variations of the versatile Chimera chassis. From the solid platform on the Griffon, its crew can achieve an impressively high rate of fire from the heavy mortar. The Griffon is tailored to provide close to medium-range mobile artillery support.

Griffon Heavy Mortar: Heavy mortars are simple barrage weapons that lob explosive shells onto enemy positions.

Range	Strength	AP	Type
12"-48"	6	4	Ordnance Barrage 1, Large Blast*

*A Griffon heavy mortar cannot fire directly.

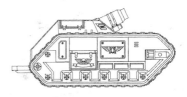

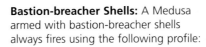

MANTICORE ROCKET LAUNCHER

The Manticore is a mobile multiple rocket launcher capable of firing devastating barrages over incredible ranges. A Manticore can be armed with a variety of different rockets but the most common remains a rack of deadly Storm Eagle rockets – the signature payload of these ancient siege vehicles. These rockets carry a lethal cluster-bomb payload and are capable of laying waste to enemy formations deployed over a large area. Once fired, these rockets soar towards their target at a blistering speed, leaving smoking contrails in their wake. Several warheads separate from the main rocket at the apex of their trajectory, before impacting amongst the foe in a series of devastating explosions. Troops abandon their positions and tank crews flee from their vehicles in a futile attempt to outrun the rockets and escape certain destruction. Some opponent have even been known to attempt to shoot a Manticore's rockets out of the air, in a desperate and foolhardy endeavour to survive.

It is a long, time-consuming process to reload a Manticore and for this reason it is rare to field them outside of dedicated artillery regiments. Whilst extremely powerful, the Manticore is also extremely unpredictable. Unless the proper blessings are applied the temperamental machine spirit within each may be offended, leading to rockets veering from their intended target or even failing to detonate. More common is the Manticore's weapon system jamming and rockets being unable to launch. In very rare circumstances it has been know for a Manticore to unintentionally fire its entire rocket payload at once in a spectacularly devastating volley that annihilates entire armies.

As such each Manticore is continuously tended to by a group of the artillery company's attendant Techpriests. In exceptional circumstances, a Manticore may be attached to an Imperial Guard infantry or armoured company. Many Imperial Guard commanders are willing to gamble on the Manticore's unpredictable nature, knowing full well that a single salvo of Storm Eagle rockets can pack the same punch as an entire artillery battery.

It is said that during the Siege of the Granitine Bastion the defenders issued their unconditional surrender at the mere sight of a trio of Manticores rather than face the inevitable bombardment. The Granitine Bastion was flattened by a barrage of rockets moments later.

	BS	Armour			Type
		F	S	R	
Manticore	3	12	10	10	Tank

Special Rules

Limited Ammunition: A Manticore Rocket Launcher typically carries a rack of four rockets. Make a note each time a rocket is fired. Once the Manticore Rocket Launcher has fired four times it has run out of ammunition. It cannot be re-armed and hence cannot be fired again during the same game. Note that only a single rocket can be fired by a Manticore Rocket Launcher each turn.

Wargear

Storm Eagle Rockets: A Manticore Rocket Launcher fires deadly Storm Eagle rockets. Each rocket delivers multiple high-explosive warheads into the heart of enemy formations, detonating with devastating effects.

Range	Strength	AP	Type
24"- 120"	10	4	Ordnance Barrage D3*, Large Blast

Roll each time the Manticore Rocket Launcher fires.

The Manticore proved pivotal during the Third War for Armageddon. General Kurov ordered the 17th Cadian Expeditionary Force to assault the Orks at Hades Rok, but knew that were Basilisks to commence a bombardment the enemy would target and destroy the artillery pieces as soon as their presence was revealed. Instead, he tasked Manticores to engage the Rok. Where Basilisks would only have had the opportunity to fire a single shell, each Manticore was modified to unleash its entire payload in one earth-shattering salvo. The Orks were caught by surprise, and a breach was opened in their defences through which the infantry of the 17th Cadian attacked, and captured the Rok.

DEATHSTRIKE MISSILE LAUNCHER

Deathstrike missiles boast an extreme payload size and a reach unparalleled by any other artillery unit. They fire an inter-continental solid fuel rocket, which has an operational range measured in thousands of kilometres. However, Deathstrike Missile Launchers have become an increasingly rare sight on Imperium battlefields, the size and logistics of their deployment seeing them overlooked in favour of more mobile artillery units. Due to their size and destructive potential, Deathstrike Missile Launchers are only deployed when the total oblivion of a key target is required.

Deathstrike missiles are able to carry a range of payloads, ranging from biological pathogens to specialised titan-hunting rockets. The most rare and destructive of all are the dreaded vortex warheads – weapons created during the Dark Age of Technology with the ability to tear the boundaries between dimensions and create a raging void of destruction that annihilates anything in its path. These warheads are only ever deployed in the most apocalyptic battles where their use has been authorised by Segmentum Command.

By far the most common payload for a Deathstrike missile is a plasma warhead. When one of these gigantic missiles detonate everything caught in the blast is engulfed by a raging fireball that vapourises flesh in an instant. There is no escape from the cataclysmic explosion as everything, even buildings, are torn apart. So armed, a Deathstrike Missile Launcher has the capability of annihilating entire armies.

| | BS | Armour | | | Type |
		F	S	R	
Deathstrike	3	12	12	10	Tank

Special Rules

T-Minus five minutes to launch... and counting:
Preparing a Deathstrike missile to fire is a lengthy and time-consuming process, during which the weapon is vulnerable to the enemy. A Deathstike missile may not be fired on the first turn of the game or if the Deathstrike Missile Launcher has moved that turn. When firing, roll a dice and apply the following modifiers:

Each full game turn the Deathstrike Missile Launcher has been on the table	**+1**
Each weapon destroyed result allocated to the Deathstrike missile whilst preparing to fire	**-1**
The Deathstrike Missile Launcher received any crew stunned or crew shaken results during the previous turn	**-1**

If the result is a **6** or more, the Deathstrike Missile can be fired. Note that a natural 6 will always result in the missile firing, regardless of negative modifiers.

Note that the Deathstrike Missile cannot be destroyed by a weapon destroyed result, only delayed. Similarly a crew stunned or crew shaken result does not necessarily prevent a Deathstike missile from launching.

Wargear
Deathstrike Missile: Few weapons unleash the same devastation as a Deathstrike missile.

Range	Strength	AP	Type
12"-960"	10	1	Ordnance Barrage, One Shot Only, D3+3" Blast*

The Deathstrike missile cannot fire directly. The weapon has a variable blast radius. Once the final position of the missile has been determined, mark the impact point with a counter and roll to determine the blast radius. All models within range of the impact point are hit. Note that as the blast does not have a 'centre of blast' and its full Strength of 10 is used for armour penetration. Cover saves may not be taken against hits caused by a Deathstrike missile.

In 994.M40, Ork Lootas infiltrated the Army 52 artillery park and stole one of three Deathstrike Missile Launchers. How this was achieved was the subject of a two-year investigation in which a dozen generals were executed for dereliction of duty. The Orks used the launcher shortly after it was taken during the battle for Baric Six. The cataclysmic explosion accounted for the destruction of two entire armoured companies of the Mordian 278th, the Baneblade *Steel Might* and over a hundred surprised Orks.

VALKYRIE ASSAULT CARRIER

The Valkyrie Assault Carrier is a twin-engine attack craft used for aerial insertions and drop missions. Screaming across a battlefield, a Valkyrie aircraft deploys its cargo into the fray, providing a deadly torrent of covering fire as the troopers within disembark.

With a few notable exceptions, Valkyries are under the control of the Imperial Navy and are attached to Imperial Guard regiments on an as need basis. Whilst the Valkyrie is operating in concert with the Imperial Guard, the aircraft's pilot reports directly to the regiment's senior officer. If Valkyries are attached to ground forces for any extended duration of time, the armour plating of the aircrafts are commonly reinforced. Whilst the added weight restricts the ability to operate at the highest altitudes, the extra protection a vital necessity if the aircraft is to survive insertion missions into heavily defended enemy positions.

A Valkyrie utilises vectored engines for vertical take-off and landings. It can even hover whilst troops deploy via rappelling lines. On occasions it is not possible for a Valkyrie to fly low or slow enough for troops to disembark in the normal manner. In such situations the passengers may jump from the aircraft's back ramp and descend using grav-chutes – a dangerous method of deployment, even for those who have trained extensively in their use. Some troopers plummet to their doom, impacting with the ground at fatal velocities.

Having inserted troops to the battlefield, Valkyries are tasked with providing supporting fire. They carry a fearsome array of anti-personnel rockets that can shatter entire formations. Lethal strafing runs leave a trail of destruction in their wake.

Vendetta Gunship
The Valkyrie can be outfitted with a wide variety of weapon payloads, one of which is dubbed the Vendetta. Multiple lascannon hard points allow the Vendetta to function as a dedicated gunship, often formed into roving search-and-destroy wings that hunt enemy battle tank formations.

	BS	Armour F	S	R	Type
Valkyrie	3	12	12	10	Fast, Skimmer
Vendetta	3	12	12	10	Fast, Skimmer

Transport
A Valkyrie has a transport capacity of twelve models. It cannot carry Ogryns.

Fire Points: None.

Access Points: Valkyries have one access point on each side of the hull and one at the rear.

Special Rules
Deep Strike, Scout.

Grav Chute Insertion: If the Valkyrie has moved flat out, passengers may still disembark, but they must do so as follows. Nominate any point over which the Valkyrie or Vendetta moved over and deploy the squad as if it were deep striking onto that point. If the unit scatters, every model must immediately take a dangerous terrain test. If any of the models cannot be deployed, the unit is destroyed as described in the 1-2 result on the Deep Strike Mishap table.

Wargear
Hellstrike Missiles: Hellstrike Missiles combine a solid fuel core with a high explosive payload.

Range	Strength	AP	Type
72"	8	3	Ordnance 1, One Shot

Multiple Rocket Pod: Multiple rocket pods contain a cluster of short-fused super-frag missiles fired in a salvo.

Range	Strength	AP	Type
24"	4	6	Heavy 1, Large Blast

Hellfury Missiles: Hellfury missiles are packed with incendiary submunitions to drive enemy troops from cover.

Range	Strength	AP	Type
72"	4	5	Heavy 1*, Large Blast, One Shot

Cover saves may not be taken against hits from a Hellfury Missile.

LORD CASTELLAN CREED & COLOUR SERGEANT KELL

The boy who was to become Lord Castellan Ursarkar E. Creed of Cadia was found in the war-wracked ruins of Kasr Gallan by soldiers of the 8th Cadian Regiment. The boy they found held an old and battered pistol in one hand and in the other was clutched a tattered, dog-eared book – the words 'De Gloria Macharius' faded on its cracked spine. He would not speak of the horrors he had endured nor how long he had survived. He was weak from starvation but still his eyes burned with a steely determination and faith in the Emperor.

Impressed by his courage, the 8th Cadian Regiment adopted the orphan and soon he was inducted into the ranks of the Whiteshield corps. It was here that the brooding Creed met a garrulous soldier by the name of Jarran Kell and the two forged a bond that was to last for the rest of their lives.

Creed proved to be a masterful strategist, mixing resolute defence with blistering counter-attacks. Creed was a natural leader as capable of commanding a platoon as he was an entire army. He had an innate grasp of tactical command and demonstrated a natural genius when devising tactics, the like of which has not been seen in the Imperium for many generations. Creed exuded an intensity that compelled obedience from all around him, complementing the iron discipline characteristic of all Cadians. It was not long before he was acclaimed Cadia's most successful living commander, and only his lowly origins held his career in check.

In 999.M41 a murderous plot by the forces of Chaos killed several members of the Cadian High Command. In times of such dire emergency there existed a special military rank, Lord Castellan of Cadia, bestowed for life or until the crisis was over. Creed was met with massive acclaim from the rank-and-file of the Cadian army. One by one his potential rivals stepped down in the interests of unity until the foundling boy was, by common consent, appointed the commander-in-chief of the entire Cadian military.

Where Creed is silent and calculating, Jarran Kell is roaring and scathing as only a colour sergeant can be. Kell is a fearsome fighter and Creed's right hand. He is a trusted companion who recognises that Creed is Cadia's best hope to survive the dark days ahead. Kell has made keeping Creed alive his life's work and has a multitude of wounds and scars to prove it. Kell is rarely away from Creed's side; his booming, amplified voice drowns out the war cries of the enemy and ensures that Creed's orders are obeyed in the heat of battle.

Supreme Commander: Creed can issue up to four orders each turn. He has a command radius of 24". Creed can use the *Bring It Down!*, *Fire on my Target!* and *Get Back in the Fight!* orders described on page 30, as well as the *First Rank, FIRE! Second Rank, FIRE!*, *Incoming!* and *Move! Move! Move!* orders described on page 36. In addition, Creed can use the following unique order:

> **For the Honour of Cadia!** Through a combination of inspiring diatribe and threatening bellows, Creed exhorts his soldiers forward, to glory!
>
> If the order is successfully issued, the ordered unit is inspired and immediately charges into the fray with little thought for its own safety. Until the end of the turn, the ordered unit has the Fearless and Furious Charge special rules – place a counter or other suitable marker next to the unit to show this.

Special Rules (Kell)

Listen Up, Maggots! If Kell is in the same unit as an officer, Leadership tests for that officer's orders can be taken on the officer's Leadership, not that of the squad receiving the order.

Sworn Protector: If Creed and Kell are in the same unit, Kell gains the Look Out – Arghh! rule as detailed on page 31.

	WS	BS	S	T	W	I	A	Ld	Sv
Ursarkar Creed	4	4	3	3	3	3	3	10	4+
Jarran Kell	4	4	3	3	2	4	2	8	4+

Special Rules (Creed)

Tactical Genius: During deployment, choose a single infantry or vehicle unit in your army. That unit has the Scouts special rule for the duration of the battle.

KNIGHT COMMANDER PASK

Knight Commander Pask is Cadia's most renowned tank ace. He has an innate understanding of armoured warfare and has commanded Leman Russ Battle Tanks through a hundred campaigns – his reputation growing with each victory.

Pask is a natural tank hunter. There is not an armoured vehicle that he has not duelled with and bested. Pask has an eye for his opponent's weak spots and his aim is such that he can send a battle cannon shell hurtling through vulnerable armour joins to detonate ammunition or fuel reserves hidden beneath, destroying the tank from the inside out.

Pask first demonstrated this uncanny ability when he was drafted to serve as part of the tank crew of the Leman Russ *Hand of Steel*. The Cadian 423rd Armoured Regiment was deployed as part of the Imperial army group raised to repulse Waaagh! Gutcutta on the planet of Cyris. When an Ork Bonecruncha ploughed over the *Hand of Steel,* its giant Deff Rolla crushed the turret and ground its commander to a paste. Pask assumed command of the battered tank and ordered the rugged machine to be turned around. With the Ork warmachine still grinding through the Imperium's lines, Pask demonstrated the talent for which he would become famous. A lascannon shot struck a poorly welded armour join on the Bonecruncha's rear and its crude engines detonated, sending the machine flipping over its own Deff Rolla in a blaze of fire and smoke. Under Pask's command

the battered *Hand of Steel* claimed another fourteen confirmed armour-kills, breaking the back of Warlord Gutcutta's assault.

During Pask's victory against the Eldar on Haytor's Hole, the repaired *Hand of Steel* was wrecked whilst engaging a squadron of Fire Prisms and, despite the Techpriest's ministrations, was declared unsalvageable. Pask was offered command of a mighty Baneblade in its stead. However, the Cadian refused and, in a ritual that has been repeated a dozen times since, insisted on putting his faith in another Leman Russ, re-naming his new steed *Hand of Steel.*

The Knight Commander was instrumental during the Saint Cyllia massacres in which Pask and his company claimed no less than four Titan-class kills. Pask himself accounted for the dreaded *Damnation Eternus*. A single battle cannon shell punched through the Titan's black torso and breached the tainted core of its plasma reactor. The resultant meltdown consumed the cursed machine in a cataclysmic explosion that set the sky on fire.

Over the decades Pask has commanded all variants of the Leman Russ and has mastered them all. He knows the capabilities and limits of each and every weapon system these mighty behemoths can mount and it is a brave fool indeed who strays into his gun-sights.

Special Rules

Leman Russ Tank Ace: Pask is always bought as an upgrade and starts the game as a commander of a Leman Russ tank (see the army list). Use the tank ace model of Pask to represent which Leman Russ he is commanding.

Pask's Leman Russ can use his Ballistic Skill of 4.

If the Leman Russ suffers a vehicle destroyed result, then Pask is slain.

Crack Shot: Provided Pask's Leman Russ remained stationary during the Movement phase, all shots made by Pask's Leman Russ that turn benefit from the Crack Shot rule.

If using the Crack Shot rule when firing against a vehicle, all shots add +1 to any armour penetration rolls.

If using the Crack Shot rule when firing at a monstrous creature, any hits that failed To Wound may be re-rolled.

"Target sighted! Red Corsairs Predator, left of the bunker. See the repair seam on the turret? Steady. Fire! Good shot. Driver, AT mines, steer left now. Gunner! Enemy infantry in crater, eleven o'clock. High explosive, fire! Sponson gunners keep an eye out, there's plenty more where they came from..."

Internal comm log, 'Hand of Steel', Operation Retort (second assault on Fort Lycoss).

SERGEANT BASTONNE

Lukas Bastonne was born of one of Cadia's noble families, his lineage guaranteeing him a prestigious career as an officer in the Imperial Guard. However, the young Bastonne eschewed his privileges and embraced the life of a common Guardsman, driven by a passion that bordered on the fanatical. Possessing a sound tactical mind, Bastonne was able to assess and adapt his squad's movement and target priorities on a continuous basis and it was not long before he was promoted to sergeant. Bastonne led his men to many heroic victories, including the Defence of Bloodhaven, the destruction of the Manthral Land-Fortress and a score more high profile battles. Bastonne is seen as the epitome of professional soldiery and self-sacrifice, a role-model that all Cadians can aspire to emulate. His chiselled features are now the public image of the Shock Troop regiments and his face is the most recognisable on the whole of Cadia. Bastonne's personal examples of courage and valour have earned him the unconditional respect of both his peers and his superiors, as well as the adoration of the masses of Cadian citizenry.

Bastonne is both blessed, and cursed, to possess an almost perfect memory. He can instantly recall past battlefield situations and combat experiences with absolute clarity. Bastonne can also recollect each and every Guardsman who has died under his command. If such things affect him he gives no outward sign, but some whisper that the faces of his dead troops torture him in his nightmares. It is even rumoured that beneath his neatly pressed, high-collared dress-uniform, Bastonne's skin is riddled with tattoos – the names of every fallen comrade inscribed unto his flesh lest his uncanny memory fail him and he forgets the brave souls' sacrifice and the events that led to their demise.

Sergeant Bastonne follows an unsurpassed ethos of duty and honour that both impresses and intimidates his comrades. He has carried out every single order and completed every mission he has ever been tasked with. Bastonne displayed this tenacity during the rescue of the Imperial Governor from the plague-ravaged world of Agrippina. Despite being vastly outnumbered, Bastonne and a squad of Cadia's finest Veterans fought their way through the shuffling masses of Plaguebearers to extract the planet's leader. Bastonne refused to leave any of his men behind and re-entered the capital hive-spire to locate a wounded trooper and drag him back to the shuttle. Upon Bastonne's return to Cadia, a parade was organised and the tales of his heroism were broadcast across the sector. The ranks of the Whiteshield companies swelled as eager youths flocked to sign up. The sergeant was awarded the Star of Terra; the highest possible achievement for a soldier to obtain in his own lifetime. What was not revealed was that Bastonne was forced to execute the very Guardsman he had gone to such lengths to save after he showed signs of sickness on the return voyage – one more face to haunt his dreams, one more name to avenge.

	WS	BS	S	T	W	I	A	Ld	Sv
Lukas Bastonne	4	4	3	3	1	3	2	10	4+

Special Rules

It's Up to Us, Lads: After all other orders have been issued, Bastonne can attempt to issue a single order to his own squad. He can use the *Bring It Down!* and *Fire on my Target!* orders described on page 30, as well as the *First Rank, FIRE! Second Rank, FIRE!*, *Incoming!* and *Move! Move! Move!* orders described on page 36.

Never Give Up, Never Surrender! As long as Sergeant Lukas Bastonne is alive, if falling back, his squad can always attempt to regroup, regardless of any normal restrictions.

"A good soldier obeys without question.
A good officer commands without doubt."

Sergeant Lukas Bastonne
quoting from the Tactica Imperium
(broadcast throughout Cadian training fortresses).

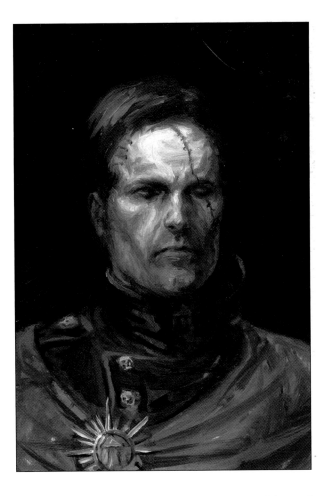

COLONEL 'IRON HAND' STRAKEN

Straken has survived decades of war, working his way from a common trooper, to the rank of Colonel of an entire regiment, the Catachan II. It was whilst Straken was still a grizzled sergeant that he earned the bionic replacement that would become both his trademark and his moniker. Whilst stalking an Eldar patrol Straken was savagely attacked by a Miral land shark that tore off his arm. By all rights Straken should have died from his injuries, but he is no normal man, he was born and bred on Catachan and is one of the toughest breed of warriors ever to serve in the Imperial Guard. Straken boasts that instead of crying like some newborn he ripped the shark's throat out with his own teeth, but some sceptics believe it more likely that he is referring to his Catachan 'Fang' knife.

Straken's list of victories is impressive indeed; the Battle of Moden's Ridge, the Dulma'lin Cleansing, the Ulani Aftermath and the fight for Vartol City are just a few of his career's more prominent campaigns. In many of these wars Straken served under the esteemed Colonel Greiss. Straken still follows his old predecessor's example and refuses to fight anywhere other than at the front line. He can be found wherever the fighting is thickest, standing shoulder to shoulder beside his men where his orders can be heard and his weapons can continue to smite the Emperor's enemies. Straken is a loud, bombastic commander with a cavalier, gung-ho attitude. He rarely stops barking out orders, yelling insults, curses and other words of encouragement to his troops. Straken's command ethic is simple – get stuck in. Straken is indifferent to danger and his confidence in both his own abilities and those of his men is unshakeable.

Straken has earned the respect of the entire regiment for his prowess in combat, his use of resourceful and innovative tactics, and his refusal to sacrifice his men for trivial gains. He has little regard for those commanders in neatly pressed uniforms that send their troops into pointless meat-grinders just to win a new medal, a fact that has led to friction when the Catachan II serve alongside regiments from other worlds.

As Straken fights for his men, so too do they fight for him. He refuses to leave a wounded man behind and famously dragged a crippled trooper halfway across the continent of Martark on Ulani IV without once breaking stride or lowering his aim. When Straken himself has suffered a severe wound his men have always managed to carry his broken form back to friendly lines. Straken has received many injuries during his years of service and his body is now riddled with cybernetic replacements and bionic implants. It appears that nothing can keep the Colonel away from the front and as long as the medicaes can continue to patch him back together, he will continue to show his troops 'how to fight the Emperor's enemies like real soldiers' accompanied with yells of 'do I have to do everything myself?'

	WS	BS	S	T	W	I	A	Ld	Sv
Colonel Straken	5	4	6	4	3	3	3	9	3+

Special Rules

Gung-ho: Colonel Straken has the Fearless universal special rule, as does his Command Squad.

Senior Officer: Straken can issue up to two orders each turn. He has a command radius of 12". Straken can use the *Bring it Down!*, *Fire on my Target!* and *Get Back in the Fight!* orders described on page 30, as well as the *First Rank, FIRE! Second Rank, FIRE!*, *Incoming!* and *Move! Move! Move!* orders described on page 36.

Cold Steel and Courage: Friendly units within 12" of Straken have the Counter-attack and Furious Charge universal special rules. This includes Colonel Straken and his Command Squad.

Man of Adamantium: Colonel Straken's extensive bionics grants him resilience and strength beyond that of an ordinary man, as shown in his profile above. In addition, Straken's close combat attacks ignore armour saves and roll an additional D6 for armour penetration.

> "Damn it, follow me, I'll show you how it's done."
>
> Colonel Straken at the Battle of Moden's Ridge.

GUARDSMAN MARBO

Guardsman Marbo is a natural born survivor and a veritable one-man army. He is the ultimate soldier and possesses skills that surpass any of the Imperium's highly trained operatives. Despite his unparalleled abilities his commanders inwardly feel there is 'something deeply wrong with the boy'.

Mysterious and aloof, little is known of Marbo's origins and most of what is told remains rumour and speculation. It is said that he was one of ten brothers who were inducted into the Catachan XII Regiment, and that during fighting against Waaagh! Urgok on Ryza all were killed. However, tales abound of a lone Guardsman returning two weeks later with the head of the Ork Warlord, a single bullet hole clearly visible between the greenskin's eyes.

The myth of Guardsman Marbo has become legendary amongst the Catachan regiments, although their tradition of exaggeration is equally well known. On Pardus it is said that Marbo destroyed an enemy armoured convoy by booby-trapping an entire ravine and on Bask's World he captured Command Post Four-Twelve single-handed, slaying the alien leader and all of its tentacled bodyguards. If half the stories about Marbo's exploits were true then he would have a collection of medals that would rival that of a Warmaster. Whatever the truth, it is without doubt that Marbo is a man who has been through hell and back too many times to remain completely sane. The blood and death he has

witnessed have warped Marbo to the point where he can only function with a blade in his hand. His eyes are empty when he isn't stalking the foe and his actions lacklustre unless he is carving his name into an enemy's chest.

Guardsman Marbo is a loner who sticks to the darkness at all times, even when he is receiving his orders at friendly outposts. Few have seen his face and none have heard him speak. He is utterly silent and acknowledges orders with but a slight nod before vanishing once more to find the enemy.

Marbo is a patient hunter. He waits in ambush until his quarry is in his sights before killing it with contemptuous ease. He is a master at blending into his surroundings and covering any trace of his whereabouts so that the enemy has no idea from where the attack is coming from. Having slit the throats of his foes he melts back into the shadows and stealthily repositions to another vantage point. In this way he throws the enemy army into utter disarray as they frantically try to locate the killer in their midst. In battle it is said that fighting Marbo is like fighting a shadow. Enemy commanders have sworn that such attacks cannot be the result of a single man and that an entire army must have ambushed them. His skills are such that it is said during the Octavius War Marbo hunted the chameleonic Lictors. If this is true Marbo gives no sign. He simply stares vacantly into space until given his next assignment by his superiors.

	WS	BS	S	T	W	I	A	Ld	Sv
Guardsman Marbo	5	5	3	3	2	5	4	7	5+

Special Rules
Fearless, Fleet, Hit and Run, Move Through Cover, Stealth.

Loner: Marbo does not take orders – any order issued to him will automatically fail.

He's Behind You! Marbo's skill at infiltration are second to none in the Imperial Guard. Marbo always starts the game in reserve, even in missions that do not normally use this rule. When Marbo becomes available he is placed anywhere on the battlefield that is more than 1" away from any enemy model. Marbo may not move or assault in the turn he arrives, although he can shoot normally.

Wargear
Ripper Pistol: Loaded with armour piercing, envenomed rounds, Marbo's ripper pistol is the final word in terminal close encounters.

Range	Strength	AP	Type
12"	X	2	Pistol, Sniper

Envenomed Blade: Marbo carries a large Catachan knife coated with deadly toxins. Guardsman Marbo's close combat attacks are Poisoned (2+).

GUNNERY SERGEANT HARKER

All Catachans have a reputation for being tough, but 'Stonetooth' Harker is perhaps the hardest of the bunch. It is said that instead of tobacco he chews glass and that he can endure pain like no other man. He can place his hands in searing flames without flinching, and shrug off knife cuts and gun wounds without a grimace. As far as 'Stonetooth' is concerned pain, and even bleeding, are concepts for weedier soldiers. Harker is a giant of a man, his large frame covered with slabs of muscle and sinew. His strength is such that he carries his heavy bolter, 'Payback', as easily as a normal man might carry a rifle, without even breaking a sweat.

Harker is uncomplaining in the completion of his duties. He shows an enthusiasm for war that is seen by Guardsmen from other regiments as somewhere between arrogance and bravado. Harker is a tough and grizzled sergeant with guts for brains. When it comes to war 'Stonetooth' is an expert, but given the chance of fighting or thinking his way out of a tight spot, Harker reaches for Payback every time.

> "Back home, I once fancied me a pair of Catachan Devil boots. Killed me half a dozen of the great ugly critters but never found a single one that wore any!"
>
> 'Stonetooth' Harker, to a doubtful Munitorum staffer.

Harker has survived the most gruelling campaigns and has yet to find an enemy that won't die to the bark of his heavy bolter or the sharpened edge of his combat blade. There isn't an aspect of war he has not mastered. From rescue missions to assassinations, reconnaissance to demolitions – Harker and his squad will get the job done. Harker leads a squad of Catachan Devils, exceptional warriors even by the exacting standards of their birth world. The nickname is a reference to the voracious predators of their world. Comprised of the regiment's bravest veterans, Harker's team take the fight directly to the enemy. They are formed to make long-range penetration raids deep behind enemy lines and when the enemy is engaged they bear the brunt of the bloody combat.

	WS	BS	S	T	W	I	A	Ld	Sv
Gunnery Sergeant Harker	4	4	4	3	1	3	2	8	5+

Special Rules:

Feel No Pain, Relentless: Note that these special rules apply only to Harker, not other members of his squad.

Catachan Devils: Harker and his squad have the Infiltrate, Stealth and Move Through Cover universal special rules.

Whilst fighting the tendrils of Tyranid Hive Fleet Leviathan on the twilight world of Jorn V, Harker's squad was ambushed by a pack of Raveners, monstrous organisms that had burrowed beneath the planet's black surface. Harker's own ammunition loader was torn apart in a flurry of claws before a scream had a chance to leave his lips and the remaining squad members were engaged in a grim fight for their lives. Harker leapt upon the closest beast without pause and wrapped his massive biceps around the alien's throat. The Ravener writhed and tried to buck him off but Harker's grip would not slacken. Harker squeezed until, with an audible crack, the creature's neck was shattered and its serpentine body finally lay still. Harker then hefted his heavy bolter from its tripod stand and opened fire on the remaining Tyranids. Each organism burst apart as the explosive bolts did their work. His dead comrades avenged, Harker dusted himself off, slung a belt of ammunition over each shoulder and stalked off to find the rest of his company, Payback tracking back and forth like a hound searching for prey.

COMMISSAR YARRICK

Commissar Yarrick is one of the greatest heroes in the entire Imperium. Although he was already a veteran of a dozen campaigns, it was during the Second War for Armageddon that the Commissar rose to fame – fighting against the largest Ork Waaagh! the Imperium had ever faced and the most dangerous of all Ork Warlords, Ghazghkull Thraka.

It was Yarrick who kept the battered defenders of Hades Hive together throughout Ghazghkull's repeated assaults. The Commissar's dogged belief in victory inspired the Imperial Guardsmen to prodigious acts of sacrifice and courage. Indeed, so motivated were the soldiers in Yarrick's presence that not a single soldier was executed for cowardice, even in the face of overwhelming odds. Yarrick's masterful leadership thwarted the Orks' attempts to storm Hades Hive time and time again and his efforts in delaying Ghazghkull proved to be the turning point in the war.

Commissar Yarrick was always found on the frontlines and suffered many wounds during the defence of Hades Hive, most notably when he fought Warboss Ugulhard single-handed. The massive greenskin severed the Commissar's arm at the elbow with a snapping battle klaw. Fighting through the pain and shock, Yarrick beheaded the Warboss with a single sweep of his chainsword before calmly reaching down and plucking the battle klaw from the Ork's twitching body

and holding it aloft for all to see. The Orks retreated in horror as the defenders of Hades Hive leapt upon the aliens with indomitable vigour. Only when the Orks were repulsed did Yarrick allow himself the luxury of passing out.

> *"Humies is all weak scum that deserve ta get stomped. 'Cept for One-Eye Yarrick. He knows how ter fight."*
>
> Warlord Ghazghkull Mag Uruk Thraka

Knowing how the Ork mind worked, Yarrick seized upon their superstitious nature. Playing with their primitive fears. Yarrick's reputation spread like wildfire, and a belief grew amongst the greenskins that he could not be killed, possessing as he did the 'evil eye' that could slay an Ork at a mere glance. To this end, he had the battle klaw modified into a prosthetic limb to replace his lost arm. Later, he lost his left eye in a firefight and had it replaced with an implant that could fire a powerful laser – if the Orks thought he had the evil eye, by the Emperor, an evil eye he would have!

Without Commissar Yarrick, Armageddon and all its surrounding systems would surely have been lost to the greenskins. Ever since that time Yarrick has devoted his life to ridding the Imperium of the 'Beast of Armageddon'.

	WS	BS	S	T	W	I	A	Ld	Sv
Commissar Yarrick	5	5	3	4	3	3	3	10	4+

Special Rules
Independent Character, Eternal Warrior, Aura of Discipline (see page 32).

Inspirational Hero: Yarrick's powerful oratory and legendary reputation can inspire men to feats of super-human bravery. Commissar Yarrick and his unit are Fearless, and all friendly units within 12" of Commissar Yarrick become Stubborn. In addition, on any turn in which Yarrick and his unit assault into close combat, they re-roll any failed To Hit rolls.

Iron Will: If Yarrick loses his last Wound, do not remove him but instead place him on his side. At the start of the Imperial Guard's next turn, roll a D6. On a 3+ he staggers back to his feet with a single Wound, bloody but defiant. If Yarrick would be placed in base contact with an enemy place him so that he is more than 1" from any enemy models. On a 1 or 2 even Yarrick is removed as a casualty.

Wargear:
Bale Eye: Yarrick's bale eye is a bionic implant that incorporates a powerful laser. It may be fired in the Shooting phase in addition to another weapon. The bale eye has the same profile as a hot-shot laspistol and grants Yarrick an extra Attack in close combat (already included in his profile).

Force Field: Yarrick is protected by a special force field that reduces the energy of enemy attacks. Any wounds that are allocated to Yarrick must be re-rolled.

CAPTAIN AL'RAHEM

Al'rahem is a Captain in the Tallarn 3rd 'Desert Tigers' and whilst nominally he carries the responsibilities of a company commander he entrusts such duties to a fellow subordinate and instead leads the most daring and vital elements of the attack himself. Unlike some officers, Al'rahem has a natural talent for tactical command and has never faltered when the bullets start flying and shells are falling. His calm aplomb and use of initiative are the envy of many aspiring generals.

Al'rahem leads his warriors in well-planned attacks, stalking his prey from afar before awaiting the most opportune moment to strike. Not for Al'rahem are the headlong and forlorn charges so beloved by many of his contemporaries. Al'rahem chooses to employ cunning and patience to win his victories, spending many days to test and probe the enemy's defences, exploiting any weakness found. When the Desert Tigers commit to battle they strike suddenly before melting away once more, escaping the foe's retribution and awaiting their next opportunity. In this way Al'rahem's forces have vanquished foes many times greater than their own number.

During the Battle for the Ruins of Esko's Moon, Al'rahem and his Desert Raiders fought a protracted guerrilla war against the elusive Eldar, a war in which both sides were utilising a hit-and-run style of warfare. It was Al'rahem himself who broke the deadlock, claiming the head of Autarch Kaliell in a carefully constructed crossfire for which the Tallarn commander and a hand-picked platoon of Desert Raiders trekked half-way across the moon's equatorial continent to strike at the ruin's lightly defended and supposedly unapproachable southern pass.

Al'rahem is both a natural leader and a gifted linguist. When combined with his charismatic charm and quick intellect it is not surprising that Al'rahem instils the respect and confidence of not only the natives of Tallarn, but of any Imperial Guard regiment allied with the Desert Tigers. It is said that Al'rahem could inspire men to follow him into the very fires of hell and even allied Catachan warriors, who are renowned for their distrust and scorn of off-worlders, have a high regard for the Tallarn commander.

Scattered tales exist of a another gifted Tallarn commander who marched across the battlefield at the behest of fabled Macharius. If the legends are believed, this commander purged the Daemon-infested world of Thoth with but a single company of Desert Raiders, supported by native tribesmen who united under the Tallarn's leadership. Some believe Al'rahem was named after this man, others argue that he is the descendent of this great hero. There are even those who insist that Al'rahem and the legendary Tallarn commander are the same man. Indeed, in a galaxy where Warpstorms and dimensional cascades can distort and twist the passage of time, who can say for sure?

	WS	BS	S	T	W	I	A	Ld	Sv
Captain Al'rahem	4	4	3	3	2	3	2	9	5+

Special Rules

Stalk the Enemy: Al'rahem and his men will track the enemy for days at a time before attacking, encircling the foe's defensive perimeters and waiting for the opportune moment. Any unit that is part of Al'rahem's Infantry Platoon must outflank.

Desert Raider: Al'rahem can issue up to two orders each turn. He has a command radius of 12". Al'rahem can use the *Bring it Down!* order, described on page 30, as well as the *First Rank, FIRE! Second Rank, FIRE!* order described on page 36. In addition, Captain Al'rahem can use the following unique order:

> **Like the Wind!** At Al'rahem's order, his followers launch a vicious attack before withdrawing and preparing to strike again.
>
> If the order is successfully issued, the ordered unit immediately makes a Shooting attack (it may not run). When this has been resolved, the unit immediately moves D6" in a direction of your choice.

Wargear

Claw of the Desert Tigers: This sword was crafted by master artisans and encrusted with emblems of the desert. The Claw of the Desert Tigers is a power weapon that inflicts instant death, regardless of the victim's Toughness.

COMMANDER CHENKOV

Commander Kubrik Chenkov is a stubborn man who refuses to admit defeat or acknowledge surrender. Like all Valhallans, Chenkov is dour and obstinate, but few of his comrades are as ruthless or as merciless.

Chenkov insists on leading the Valhallan 18th 'Tundra Wolves' from the very front, eschewing the safety of a command bunker for the battlelines where he can keep a stern eye on his troops and instil his own brand of motivation and encouragement. Any that dare to retreat within his sight are likely to find the guns of their once allies turned upon them, such is Chenkov's opinion of cowards. It is whispered that Chenkov has killed more of his own men than he has the enemy, and his bolt pistol has a fearsome reputation amongst friend and foe alike.

Chenkov does not employ subtle strategy to win his wars, relying instead on blunt, direct tactics. He knows full well that he has tens of thousands of troops at his command and that with enough manpower, any opponent can be overcome. Chenkov will willingly throw his men at the heavily defended walls of a fortress if it will eventually bring them crashing down. Should the location of an enemy leader be identified, Chenkov is likely to send in more squads to ensure the general cannot escape whilst artillery is tracking into position. His men doggedly obey the grim-faced Commander, knowing that to disobey means certain

death. So high is the attrition rate amongst the Tundra Wolves that they have been refounded more than a dozen times in recent decades. Each time, Chenkov and the few remaining survivors of the regiment, journey to lead the newly raised unfortunates.

Although unimaginative, Chenkov's tactics are doubtlessly effective. During the year-long Siege of Kotrax the Commander's actions brought a swift, if bloody, end to the conflict when he assumed command of an Imperial battle group and stormed a heavily defended citadel without armoured support or dedicated siege weapons. The conflict cost ten million Imperial Guardsmen their lives but Chenkov received the Merit of the High Lords for his achievements in liberating Kotrax in such a short span of time.

Under Chenkov's command, platoons of Guardsmen were ordered to draw enemy fire, to prevent the valued demolitions crews attempting to breach the Emrah battle-fortress from being discovered.

When the advance of Leman Russ Battle Tanks was slowed by mines during the second war for the Trenk Ravine, Chenkov used his troops to clear the explosives by marching them across the minefields. Chenkov's ruthless command style continues to win the Imperium many victories and though the cost is high, the price of failure is intolerable.

	WS	BS	S	T	W	I	A	Ld	Sv
Commander Chenkov	4	4	3	3	2	3	2	9	4+

Special Rules

Forward, You Dogs! Commander Chenkov is a ruthless tyrant whose men would rather take their chances with the enemy than his fearsome temper. All friendly units within 12" of Commander Chenkov have the Stubborn special rule. This includes Chenkov and his Command Squad.

Taskmaster: Commander Chenkov can issue up to two orders each turn. He has a command radius of 12". Commander Chenkov can use the *Get Back in the Fight!* orders described on page 30, as well as the *Move! Move! Move!* order described on page 36.

Send in the Next Wave: An army that includes Commander Chenkov may purchase this special rule for its Conscript squads, as described in the army list. A unit with this special rule can, at the start of the player's turn, be removed from play as casualties if the controlling player wishes, counting as destroyed.

Any unit with this special rule that is removed from play may be brought back into play at the beginning of the controlling player's next turn. The new unit moves onto the board from the player's board edge. The unit arrives with as many models and exactly the same armaments as its full strength predecessor – it is treated as a new, identical unit that has just arrived from reserve.

MOGUL KAMIR

Mogul Kamir is the fiercest mounted warrior of his age, a renowned warrior more daring and bloodthirsty than any of his fellow Attilans. Mogul Kamir rose to take control of his tribe by the age of thirteen, killing his uncle, the chief, in single combat. By the age of fifteen Kamir was ruler of over twenty tribes by right of conquest but still his lust for combat was not sated. The need to fight burned so brightly within Kamir's heart that he sought an even greater challenge and sought counsel with the King of Khanasan, Lord of Attila. The wise King spoke to Kamir of the glorious armies of the Imperial Guard and offered the young warrior a lifetime of battle across the galaxy, with more foes to test his skills against than could ever be found on Attila. With a grin, Kamir accepted.

Mogul Kamir lives for the thrill of battle and his taste for danger is well known. Few who fight beside him remain unmarked by blade or blast and despite the fact that many do not return, it is considered a high honour to accompany Mogul Kamir into the heat of battle. His lust for fighting is a matter of pride amongst the Attilans and only the fiercest and most skilled of warriors ride with Mogul Kamir, many of which have ritually duelled for the right.

Few Attilans escape a lifetime's battle without the telltale signs of heroic endeavour. Attilans have little respect for medals awarded after a battle's conclusion and feel that the only symbols of merit worth owning are those won in the heat of battle, whilst their warriors' blood is still hot in their veins. As such the most valued trophies of war are the scars earned from cheating death and the skull of a worthy foe. Few have a collection of such trophies as great as Mogul Kamir. His body is riddled with scar-tissue and many a warlord's skull adorns his hunting-lance, both a testament to his courage, and a proclamation of his skills as Attila's foremost warrior.

No steed was able to cope with Kamir's unquenchable battle lust and those that did not die from wounds on the battlefield died from exhaustion. Even the tough breed of Attilan warhorses were run into the ground by Kamir's constant charges and counter-attacks. The Adeptus Mechanicus crafted for Kamir a cybernetic steed that would never tire, never flinch and never bleed to death – a gift bestowed to the great Attilan warrior for his actions in saving the manufactorum world of Loxar IV from the predations of the Necrons.

Mogul Kamir has a short and violent temper, an attitude that reinforces his barbaric appearance. It is a fool indeed who fails to show the Attilan Chief the proper respect, but those that can see past the savage-looking furs and tribal scars find a courageous and cunning ally who can turn the tide of battle with a single charge.

	WS	BS	S	T	W	I	A	Ld	Sv
Mogul Kamir	4	3	3	3	2	3	3	8	5+

Special Rules

Khanasan's Fiercest: Mogul Kamir and his unit of Rough Riders have the Furious Charge ability. Whilst Mogul Kamir is alive, he and his unit are Fearless.

Vicious Temperament: Mogul Kamir's headstrong attitude often sees him recklessly charging the enemy. As long as Mogul Kamir is alive, he and his unit are subject to the Rage special rule as detailed in the Warhammer 40,000 rulebook.

Wargear

Cyber-steed: On a turn that Mogul Kamir charges he receives +D3 Attacks instead of +1.

"It is not enough that I achieve victory – my enemy must suffer total defeat. It is not enough that I kill – all my foes must die. It is not enough that I succeed – all others must fail!"

Mogul Kamir at the conclusion of the
Twenty-Third Quadrant Suppression.

NORK DEDDOG

Nork Deddog is a legend in his own lifetime, an Ogryn whose fighting abilities are almost as astonishing as his mental development. By Ogryn standards Nork is a veritable genius; he can sign his own name ("N" is fer Nork), count to four (his thumb still confuses him though), and even speak in short sentences. Such precocious development in one of his race inevitably came to the attention of the Commissars and Nork soon found himself placed on special duties.

After extensive training, Nork Deddog was assigned to the Catachan II Regiment fighting on Balor. The regiment's commander, Colonel Greiss, adopted Nork as his personal bodyguard, and the Ogryn accompanied Greiss through the four years that the war lasted. During this time the sight of Greiss and Nork became a familiar one: the ancient and bone-thin colonel bawling out his orders whilst shells burst around him and bullets ricocheted off Nork's dense skull. The Ogryn bodyguard saved Colonel Greiss's life on many occasions, most famously when he carried the badly wounded Catachan commander back from the disaster at Hill-Gamma Zero.

Nork's reputation for loyalty is unsurpassed and his skills as a bodyguard have been in high demand by Imperium officers across the sector. When Ork Warboss Uglurk Gitsmasha and a mob of his hardest Meganobz charged the Imperial Guard's command dugout, Nork Deddog was the only one

to stand his ground beside Sub-overlord Ven Vambold. Nork killed the massive greenskin Warlord with a single headbutt of such extreme violence that the remaining Orks were totally awestruck and retreated rather than face the angry Ogryn bodyguard.

Nork's own body has proven time and again to be the most effective shield an officer can have against enemy fire. Nork will do his utmost to protect his master from harm, even going so far as to throw himself in front of enemy fire. On Follax IV Nork selflessly leapt on top of an enemy grenade that would have otherwise killed Commander Richep, crushing both the grenade and the grenadier to a pulp beneath his massive bulk. The explosion that followed was muffled and Nork seemed to notice his resulting shrapnel wounds with only passing curiosity.

Nork has personally saved the lives of over a hundred officers and by doing so has been instrumental in securing victories on dozens of worlds. Nork has a large collection of medals, laurels, citations and personal gifts, including the Commissar's cap given to him by Aaron Blest that became his trademark during the Dimmamak war. It is not for trinkets or baubles that Nork Deddog continues to serve (although he is particularly proud of his big shiny buttons), but rather it is for the content feeling he gets when fighting at a friend's side.

	WS	BS	S	T	W	I	A	Ld	Sv
Nork Deddog	4	3	5	5	3	3	4	8	4+

Special Rules
Feel No Pain, Furious Charge, Stubborn, Bulky (see page 42).

Loyal to the End: Nork is extremely protective and very loyal to his commander, so much so that he (and his body odour) will stick to the officer like glue. Nork has the Look out – Arghh! rule as detailed on page 31. In addition, a Commissar (of either rank) will never shoot Nork as a result of the Summary Execution rule. If a Commissar shoots Nork's Commander, however, Nork immediately retaliates – remove the Commissar from play.

Heroic Sacrifice: Nork reacts to any threat to his master with effective, if unimaginative, bouts of violence. Should Nork lose his final Wound in close combat, the enemy unit that inflicted the wound immediately suffers D6 Strength 6 hits as Nork desperately attempts to 'smash dem wot is tryin' ta 'urt da kernul'. After the attacks have been resolved Nork slumps to the floor asking his officer 'did we win?' before passing out from his wounds – remove Nork as a casualty.

> "Da Sergeant Major asked me what my job was an' I said it was to, uh, do what I was told. He said I was a genius and gave me another medal. I likes da Imperial Guard!"
>
> Nork Deddog, Ogryn Bodyguard

WARGEAR

This section of Codex: Imperial Guard lists the weapons and equipment used by the armies of the Imperial Guard, along with the rules for using them in your games of Warhammer 40,000.

Weapons and equipment that can be used by one type of model or unit are detailed here, while equipment that is unique to a single model or unit (including wargear carried by named special characters) is detailed in the appropriate entry in the Forces section. We have included page numbers for quick reference. For example, lasguns are ubiquitous and carried by many models, and so are detailed in this section. The ripper gun, however, is unique to Ogryns, and is therefore detailed in the Ogryns entry.

WEAPONS

Autocannon: Autocannons fire large calibre, high velocity shells at a prodigious rate. They are the heavy weapon of choice for commanders facing large infantry formations and lightly armoured vehicles.

Range	Strength	AP	Type
48"	7	4	Heavy 2

Boltgun: The boltgun, or 'bolter', is a rare and devastating weapon amongst the ranks of the Imperial Guard. It fires self-propelled missiles or 'bolts' that explode upon penetrating its target, blowing it apart from the inside.

Range	Strength	AP	Type
24"	4	5	Rapid Fire

Bolt Pistol: Bolt pistols are smaller versions of bolters. Favoured amongst the ranks of officers and Commissars, they are a potent symbol of status as well as a lethal side arm.

Range	Strength	AP	Type
12"	4	5	Pistol

Demolition Charge: Small, compact, but extremely destructive, demolition charges are used to destroy fortifications and enemy armour emplacements.

Range	Strength	AP	Type
6"	8	2	Assault 1, Large Blast, One Shot Only

Eviscerator: . . . . .See page 35

Flamer: Flamers spew out gouts of volatile promethium that instantly ignites and immolates those caught in the superheated conflagration.

Range	Strength	AP	Type
Template	4	5	Assault 1

Force Weapon: See the Warhammer 40,000 rulebook.

Frag Grenades: See the Warhammer 40,000 rulebook.

Grenade Launcher: Grenade launchers are versatile, man-portable weapons capable of firing a range of deadly rounds.

Each time the grenade launcher fires, the controlling player can decide which round is being used.

Frag Grenade

Range	Strength	AP	Type
24"	3	6	Assault 1, Blast

Krak Grenade

Range	Strength	AP	Type
24"	6	4	Assault 1

Heavy Bolter: An enormous version of the bolter, the heavy bolter fires fist-sized bolts at the enemy with a staggering rate of fire.

Range	Strength	AP	Type
36"	5	4	Heavy 3

Heavy Flamer: The heavy flamer is the weapon of choice for sweeping fortifications clear and purging the ranks of the enemy.

Range	Strength	AP	Type
Template	5	4	Assault 1

Hot-shot Lasgun: .See page 46

Hot-shot Laspistol: The hot-shot laspistol utilises the same high-energy technology as the hot-shot lasgun.

Range	Strength	AP	Type
6"	3	3	Pistol

Hunting Lance: . . . . .See page 44

Krak Grenades: See the Warhammer 40,000 rulebook.

Lascannon: The massive power cells required to fire a mighty lascannon is an indication of the destructive power of the weapon. The focused energy blast unleashed by this anti-tank weapon can cut through even the thickest armour.

Range	Strength	AP	Type
48"	9	2	Heavy 1

Lasgun: The ubiquitous lasgun is easy to replicate and is therefore the most common weapon in the entire Imperium. There are many subtle variations to the humble lasgun, but all are reliable and simple to maintain. Many experienced fighters prefer these trustworthy weapons to more destructive weapons for these very reasons.

Range	Strength	AP	Type
24"	3	-	Rapid Fire

Laspistol: Typically reserved for officers, the unassuming laspistol is based upon the same technology as the lasgun. The standard power packs for these weapons can be recharged from a standard power source or by exposing the cell to light or heat.

Range	Strength	AP	Type
12"	3	-	Pistol

Melta Bombs: See the Vehicles chapter of the Warhammer 40,000 rulebook for details of using meltabombs.

Meltagun: Meltaguns are short-ranged but lethal anti-armour weapons that fire a superheated stream of pure destruction. Even the thickest armour vapourises under the sub-atomic blast.

Range	Strength	AP	Type
12"	8	1	Assault 1, Melta

Missile Launcher: The missile launcher is a favoured weapon amongst heavy weapons teams due to the tactical flexibility afforded by a range of warheads.

Each time the missile launcher fires, the controlling player can decide which round is being used.

Frag missile
Range	Strength	AP	Type
48"	4	6	Heavy 1, Blast

Krak missile
Range	Strength	AP	Type
48"	8	3	Heavy 1

Mortar: Mortars are anti-personnel weapons, capable of breaking up and pinning down enemy infantry formations.

Range	Strength	AP	Type
48"	4	6	Heavy 1, Blast, Barrage

Multi-melta: A larger, more destructive version of the meltagun, perfect for reducing armoured tanks and reinforced bunkers to molten slag.

Range	Strength	AP	Type
24"	8	1	Heavy 1, Melta

Plasma Cannon: Plasma technology is rare and highly destructive, for both the enemy and the wielder. 'Bolts' of pure plasma explode upon impact with the fury of a supernova, scything through steel, flesh and bone as if it were nothing.

Range	Strength	AP	Type
36"	7	2	Heavy 1, Blast, Gets Hot!

Plasma Gun: It is a rare 'honour' to serve as a squad's plasma gunner. Whilst destructive, plasma guns are prone to overheat and few Guardsmen survive long enough to truly master these revered weapons.

Range	Strength	AP	Type
24"	7	2	Rapid Fire, Gets Hot!

Plasma Pistol: Perhaps the most destructive sidearm in common use in the Imperium, a soldier with a plasma pistol wields the power of a small sun in his hands.

Range	Strength	AP	Type
12"	7	2	Pistol, Gets Hot!

Power Fist: See the Warhammer 40,000 rulebook.

Power Weapon: See the Warhammer 40,000 rulebook.

Ripper Gun: . . . . See page 42

Servo-arm: . . . . See page 34

Shotgun: Shotguns are sturdy and versatile weapons wielded by warriors across the Imperium.

Range	Strength	AP	Type
12"	3	-	Assault 2

Snare Mines: . . . . See page 40

Sniper Rifle: There are many different sniper rifles utilised by the Imperial Guard's marksmen. Some regiments prefer to use needle sniper rifles that fire small darts made from deadly neuro-toxins. Others may use the 'long-las', a variant of the humble lasgun with a reinforced barrel and overcharged power cells.

Range	Strength	AP	Type
36"	X	6	Heavy 1, Sniper

VEHICLE ARMOURY

Battle Cannon: . . . . .See page 48

Bastion-breacher Shells: . . . . .See page 53

Camo Netting: Some vehicles carry rolls of camouflage netting that can be unrolled by the crew to help hide the vehicle from the enemy. This netting varies from relatively rare cameleoline materials to crude, but effective webbing interwoven with the local flora.

A vehicle equipped with camo netting has the Stealth universal special rule, if it remained stationary in the previous friendly Movement phase.

Chem Cannon: .See page 50

Colossus Siege Mortar: . . . . .See page 53

Deathstrike Missile: . . . . .See page 55

Demolisher Siege Cannon: . . . . .See page 49

Dozer Blade: Dozer blades are heavy, reinforced ploughs, blades, rams or scoops that are used to clear obstacles from the vehicle's path. Many dozer blades are used to help the vehicle traverse minefields that would otherwise damage the vehicles' track units.

Vehicles equipped with a dozer blade can re-roll a failed difficult terrain test.

Earthshaker Cannon: . . . . .See page 53

Enclosed Crew Compartment: . . . . .See page 52

Eradicator Nova Cannon: . . . . .See page 49

Executioner Plasma Cannon: . . . . .See page 49

Exterminator Autocannon: . . . . .See page 49

Extra Armour: Some Imperial Guard vehicle crews add additional ablative plating to their vehicles to provide extra protection from enemy attacks.

Vehicles equipped with the extra armour upgrade count crew stunned results on the Vehicle Damage table as crew shaken results instead.

Griffon Heavy Mortar: . . . . .See page 53

Heavy Stubber: Despite its lack of penetrative power the heavy stubber is still a favourite amongst some tank crews thanks to its long range and punishing rate of fire.

Range	Strength	AP	Type
36"	4	6	Heavy 3

Hellfury Missiles: . . . . .See page 56

Hellstrike Missiles: . . . . .See page 56

Hunter-killer Missile: Hunter-killer missiles are single-use weapon systems commonly fitted to Imperial vehicles allowing even lightly armoured Chimeras to engage enemy battle tanks.

A hunter-killer missile is a krak missile with unlimited range that can only be fired once per game. They are fired at Ballistic Skill 3 and are treated as an additional weapon.

Hydra Autocannon: . . . . .See page 51

Inferno Cannon: . . . . .See page 50

Medusa Siege Cannon: . . . . .See page 53

Melta Cannon: .See page 50

Multiple Rocket Pod: . . . . .See page 56

Multi-laser: The enhanced phased capacitors and reinforced barrels of a multi-laser mean that a more destructive power level can be combined with a high rate of fire, making this weapon effective against lightly armoured targets and onrushing hordes alike.

Range	Strength	AP	Type
36"	6	6	Heavy 3

Punisher Gatling Cannon: . . . . .See page 49

Searchlight: Searchlights are often fitted to Imperial Guard vehicles to cut through the darkness, so that the foe may not cower from the vehicle's sights.

Searchlights are used when the Night Fighting rule is in effect. If a vehicle has a searchlight it must still use the night fighting rules to pick a target but, having acquired a target, will illuminate it with the searchlight. For the rest of the Shooting phase, any other unit that fires at the illuminated unit does not use the Night Fighting rule. However, a vehicle that uses a searchlight, can be targeted during the following enemy turn, as if the Night Fighting rules were not in effect, as the enemy can see the searchlight.

Smoke Launchers: See the Warhammer 40,000 rulebook.

Storm Bolter: A storm bolter is a pair of linked bolters that can cut down ranks of enemies in an explosive hail of bolts.

Range	Strength	AP	Type
24"	4	5	Assault 2

Storm Eagle Rockets: . . . . .See page 54

Vanquisher Battle Cannon: . . . . .See page 49

ARMOUR

Carapace Armour: Carapace armour is made up large rigid plates of armaplas or ceramite moulded to fit the bearer.

A model with carapace armour has an armour save of 4+.

Flak Armour: Cheap and easy to produce, flak armour comprises several layers of ablative thermoplast materials and impact absorbent carbifibres.

A model with flak armour has an armour save of 5+.

Power Armour: Made from thick ceramite plates and electronically motivated fibre bundles, power armour is amongst the best protective armour available to the servants of the Imperium.

A model with power armour has an armour save of 3+

OTHER EQUIPMENT

Camo Cloaks: Some units are able to use rare cameleoline material in their armour, uniforms or as cloaks. Cameleoline automatically blends in with the surrounding terrain making the wearer much harder to spot.

A model wearing a camo cloak has the stealth universal special rule.

Medi-pack Medi-packs contain all the necessary drugs, dressings and surgical tools a field-medic requires to treat battle wounds and injuries.

Whilst the medic is still alive, his squad has the Feel No Pain universal special rule.

Platoon Standard: .See page 36

Imperial Infantryman's Uplifting Primer
Upon recruitment, many Guardsmen are issued with a copy of the Imperial Infantryman's Uplifting Primer. Within the pages of this book is invaluable advice on a score of topics, from the maintenance of a lasgun to the correct method of engaging an Ork in hand-to-hand combat. Commissars are wont to execute those troopers who deface or misplace their Primer.

Refractor Field: This is an all-enclosing energy field that partially refracts energy around the bearer, protecting him from otherwise fatal damage.

A refractor field grants the bearer a 5+ invulnerable save.

Regimental Standard: Whilst the standard bearer is still alive, his squad counts as scoring one additional wound for the purposes of calculating close combat results. In addition, any friendly units within 12" re-roll failed Morale and Pinning tests.

Rosarius: . . . . .See page 35

Vox-caster: A vox-caster is a sophisticated and reliable communications array that is connected to the Tactical command net via tight beam transmitters and a series of signal decoders.

If an officer is attempting to issue an order to a friendly unit and both the officer's Command Squad and the chosen unit contain a model with a vox-caster, the Leadership test to see if the order has been understood can be re-rolled if failed.

RAISING A REGIMENT

Listen up recruit! You're in the Imperial Guard now, the largest fighting force in the galaxy. First thing's first though, we'll need to get you through basic training, so here is some advice to help you survive boot camp.

Imperial Guard armies are characterised by the large number of soldiers, tanks and artillery they can field, from the humble Imperial Guardsman to the mighty Leman Russ Battle Tank. There are many ways to personalise your army, each unit opening up new tactical options. However, there are a few basics to bear in mind as you begin your collection.

CALL TO ARMS

The standard force organisation chart includes two essential Troops units and a single compulsory HQ choice. This means that when collecting your army the first things you will need are troops to command, and a general to lead them.

Troops are vital in games of Warhammer 40,000 as in many standard missions they are the only units that can capture objectives and secure victory. Thankfully the Imperial Guard can field a great many such units. By selecting an Imperial Guard Infantry Platoon it's possible to field well over a hundred individual models for just a single Troops choice. The sheer firepower such formations can kick out is a terrifying prospect for any opponent. Heavy Weapons squads and Special Weapons squads add an extra punch, allowing the platoon to deal with a host of enemy armoured units and large monstrous creatures. Many players opt to upgrade their squads with characters such as Commissars, who ensure the troops' mettle does not fail in the heat of battle. Alternatively, if the prospect of quite so many soldiers seems daunting, then why not consider fielding a squad of Veterans or Penal Legion. These units have access to a variety of special rules and wargear options that allow you to tailor your force into a group of combat specialists or crazed desperadoes. Regardless of what you choose, you will have plenty of soldiers to implement your strategy and complete your mission.

Imperial Guard Commanders lead from a Command Squad. These squads can enhance the effectiveness of your troops by issuing one of a selection of orders. The key to winning a game of Warhammer 40,000 might very well depend on the player's choice of which orders he issues – so choose wisely. Company Command Squads also have the option to upgrade with a variety of specialists and Regimental Advisors with unique abilities. These range from a medic who can heal wounded troops, to a Master of Ordnance who calls down mighty artillery strikes. Imperial Guard armies also have access to unique individuals such as Lord Commissars who inspire those around to great acts of courage, and Primaris Psykers who are powerful characters with deadly psychic powers.

REINFORCEMENTS

Once you've selected your HQ and Troops units, the support units become available to you. Elites, Fast Attack and Heavy Support options allow you to pick units with unique weapons and abilities. Some players will prefer to concentrate on a particular aspect of warfare but a balanced 'combined arms' force will be, for many players, the ideal way to create a force that allows them to collect elements from all parts of the army list. Here are a few examples of the more dedicated elements and compositions available to the Imperial Guard player.

The Infantry Assault Wave: The Imperial Guard has an almost inexhaustible reservoir of manpower at its disposal and players who opt to field lots of infantry regularly take several Infantry Platoons to overwhelm their opponents. These forces tend to excel at defeating small, elite armies such as Eldar or Chaos Space Marines that simply can't sustain a war of attrition. Specialist units such as Ratlings can help you to pin down the enemy, whilst Ogryns provide some much needed close combat support.

The Rapid Attack Force: Imperial Guard forces need not be slow and lumbering. Rough Riders, Storm Troopers, Sentinel Scouts and Hellhounds are able to bring the fight to the enemy. Such elements are particularly effective against armies such as the Tau who depend upon long-range firepower to secure victory. Imperial Guard Infantry Squads mounted in transport vehicles such as Chimeras or Valkyries are also able to respond to battlefield situations more quickly than their footslogging comrades.

The Armoured Blitzkrieg: The Imperial Guard have access to more vehicles than any other army in the Warhammer 40,000 game. Several Leman Russ Battle Tank and Hellhound Flame Tank patterns, Armoured Sentinels, Vendettas and Hydra Flak Tanks are all yours to command. Tank-heavy armies tend to include at least one Techpriest Enginseer, a character who can make battlefield repairs to damaged vehicles and ensure that the full might of these fearsome behemoths is maintained.

The Heavy Artillery: The Imperial Guard is reknowned for its fearsome artillery batteries. Basilisks, Medusas, Griffons, Manticores and Colossus Siege Mortars can pound any enemy into oblivion. Ordnance is ideal for destroying large blocks of enemy infantry from afar, such as Ork or Tyranid hordes that excel at close range assaults. Even heavily armoured targets such as Space Marines or enemy battle tanks are not safe, their armour little proof against the heavy bombardments. In addition, the Imperial Guard has at its disposal the ultimate doomsday device in the Warhammer 40,000 game – the dreaded Deathstrike Missile Launcher.

REGIMENTAL COLOURS

Painters will first need to decide from which planet their army was raised – not only does each regiment have its own particular background but each also has its own distinct look and uniform styles. Some players may wish to invent an entirely new regiment, with it's own traditions and fighting styles. Also, not every Imperial Guard force need contain troops from a single regiment. Some armies might be formed from the survivors of two or more disparate home worlds, allowing you to collect and paint a wide variety of models.

On the following pages you will find fabulously painted examples of many of the models in the Imperial Guard range. Some painters may wish to follow these examples, while others may use the information to inspire the invention of their own regiment. Further guidance on painting your army can be found in the 'How to Paint Citadel Miniatures' book.

Cadian Shock Troops advance through the ruins of an Imperial city.

Catachan Jungle Fighters defend an ancient outpost.

CADIAN SHOCK TROOPS

Guardsman with medi-pack.

Guardsman with vox-caster.

Company Commander.

Guardsman with regimental standard.

Guardsman with plasma gun.

Guardsmen with grenade launchers.

Guardsman with flamer.

Guardsman with meltagun.

Guardsman with plasma gun.

Armed with lasguns, the vast ranks of Guardsmen form the very backbone of the Imperial Guard.

The Sergeants of Imperial Guard Infantry Squads lead their troops into the heart of battle.

Commander with plasma pistol and power sword.

Commander with power sword.

Commander with power fist.

Commander with power sword and plasma pistol.

Commander with bolt pistol.

◀ Leman Russ Battle Tanks provide armoured firepower to Imperial Guard armies.

Guardsman with platoon standard.

Sergeants with laspistols and chainswords.

CADIAN SHOCK TROOPS

▼ Basilisks are self-propelled artillery pieces that mount an earthshaker cannon.

Heavy Weapons Team with mortar.

Heavy Weapons Team with missile launcher.

Guardsman with sniper rifle.

Heavy Weapons Team with lascannon.

Heavy Weapons Team with heavy bolter.

Guardsman with sniper rifle.

◀ Lord Castellan Ursarkar E. Creed and Colour Sergeant Jarran Kell.

Scout Sentinel with autocannon and searchlight.

Commissar with power fist.

Guardsmen with vox-casters.

Wounded Guardsman.

The Leman Russ Demolisher ▶ mounts a powerful, if short-ranged, siege cannon.

CATACHAN JUNGLE FIGHTERS

Guardsman with plasma gun.

Company Commander with boltgun.

Guardsman with medi-pack.

Guardsman with vox-caster.

Guardsman with regimental standard.

Guardsmen with heavy flamers.

Guardsmen with flamers.

Guardsmen with lasguns.

Sergeant with power sword.

Guardsman with lasgun.

Guardsman with sniper rifle.

Catachan Jungle Fighters emerge from cover to launch a deadly ambush.

Commander with
power fist.

Commander with
bolt pistol.

Commander with boltgun
and power fist.

Commander with
plasma pistol and
power sword.

Guardsman with
grenade launcher.

Guardsmen with lasguns.

Guardsmen with lasguns.

Sergeant with
boltgun.

Guardsman with
demolition charge.

Guardsman with
vox-caster.

Guardsmen with lasguns.

Leman Russ Battle ▶
Tanks bristle with
heavy firepower.

CATACHAN JUNGLE FIGHTERS

Heavy Weapons Team with lascannon.

Heavy Weapons Team with heavy bolter.

Heavy Weapons Team with missile launcher.

Heavy Weapons Team with mortar.

◀ *Guardsmen with* ▶
sniper rifles.

Chimeras are rugged armoured personnel carriers used by the Imperial Guard. ▼

Scout Sentinel with multi-laser and searchlight.

Scout Sentinel with heavy flamer.

Guardsman with shotgun.

Sergeant.

Guardsmen with lasguns.

Guardsman with vox-caster.

A Command Squad orders his Catachan Jungle Fighters to man the defences and repulse an Ork horde.

MORDIAN IRON GUARD

Heavy Weapons Team with lascannon.

Commander with bolt pistol.

Sergeant.

Guardsman with lasgun.

TALLARN DESERT RAIDERS

Sergeant with plasma pistol.

Guardsman with grenade launcher.

Captain Al'rahem.

Guardsmen with lasguns.

ARMAGEDDON STEEL LEGION

Guardsmen with lasguns.

Commander with bolt pistol and power sword.

Guardsman with lasgun.

VALHALLAN ICE WARRIORS

Guardsmen with lasguns.

Sergeant with bolt pistol.

Guardsman with lasgun.

VOSTROYAN FIRST BORN

Guardsman with
lasgun.

Guardsman with
flamer.

Company
Commander.

Guardsman with
regimental standard.

Guardsman with
sniper rifle.

Guardsman with
sniper rifle.

Commander with
power fist.

Guardsman with
plasma gun.

Guardsman with
medi-pack.

Guardsman with
lasgun.

▼ Leman Russ Battle Tank
of one of the Vostroyan
First Born regiments.

Armegeddon Steel Legion Chimera with
multi-laser and heavy bolter. ▼

Chimera of a
Vostroyan First Born
regiment, outfitted
with defensive
heavy stubber. ▼

Commissar.

Techpriest Enginseer.

▼ Valkyrie Assault Carrier with lascannon and hellstrike missiles.

▼ Valhallan Ice Warriors Leman Russ Battle Tank.

VALHALLA

Armageddon Steel Legion Armoured
Sentinel with plasma cannon.

Vostroyan First Born Armoured
Sentinel with lascannon.

Cadian Shock Troops Scout Sentinel with
missile launcher and searchlight.

Mordian Iron
Guard Hellhound
Flame Tank.

Tallarn Desert Raiders Chimera.

Techpriest Enginseer.

*Basilisk from a Vostroyan
First Born regiments.* ▶

Commissar Yarrick.

Commissar with
plasma pistol.

Lord Commissar with
power sword.

Commissar with
power fist.

Astropath.

Officer of the Fleet.

Sanctioned Psyker.

Primaris Psyker.

Master of Ordnance.

Ratling Snipers.

Ratling Snipers.

Ogryn Bone 'ead.

Ogryns armed with ripper guns.

IMPERIAL GUARD ARMY LIST

The following army list enables you to field an Imperial Guard army and fight battles using the scenarios included in the Warhammer 40,000 rulebook.

USING THE ARMY LIST

The Imperial Guard army list is split into five sections: HQ, Elites, Troops, Fast Attack and Heavy Support. All of the squads, vehicles and characters in the army are placed into one of these sections depending upon their role on the battlefield. Each model is also given a points value, which varies depending on how effective that model is in battle.

Before you choose an army, you will need to agree with your opponent upon the type of game you are going to play and the maximum total number of points each of you will spend. Then you can proceed to pick your army.

USING A FORCE ORGANISATION CHART

The army list is used in conjunction with the force organisation chart from a scenario. Each chart is split into five categories that correspond to the sections in the army list, and each category has one or more boxes. Each grey-toned box indicates that you may make one choice from that section of the army list, while a dark-toned box indicates a compulsory selection.

This army list is primarily designed for use with the Standard Missions from the Warhammer 40,000 rulebook. We have included the chart used for Standard Missions below. This army list may be used in conjunction with other missions and scenarios that use the force organisation charts, but please note that play balance may be affected if they are used for anything other than a Standard Mission.

ARMY LIST ENTRIES

Each entry in the army list represents a different unit. More information about the background and rules for the Imperial Guard and their options can be found in the Forces of the Imperial Guard section, while information and examples of the Citadel miniatures you will need to represent them can be found in the Soldiers of the Imperial Guard section.

Each unit entry in the Imperial Guard army list is split into several sections:

Unit Name: At the start of each army list entry you will find the name of the unit alongside the points cost of the unit without any upgrades.

Unit Profile: This section will show the profile of any models the unit can include.

Unit Composition: Where applicable, this section will show the number and type of models that make up the basic unit, before any upgrades are taken.

Unit Type: This section refers to the Warhammer 40,000 Unit Type Rules chapter. For example, a unit may be classed as infantry, vehicle or cavalry, which will subject it to a number of rules regarding, movement, shooting, assault etc. If the Unit Type box includes the word 'Unique' you may only include one of this unit in your army.

Wargear: This section details the weapons and equipment the models in the unit are armed with. The cost for all these models and their equipment is included in the points cost listed next to the unit name.

Special Rules: Any special rules that apply to the models in the unit are listed here. These special rules are explained in further detail in either the Forces of the Imperial Guard section or the Universal Special Rules section of the Warhammer 40,000 rulebook.

Dedicated Transport: Where applicable, this section refers to any transport vehicles the unit may take. These have their own army list entry on page 99. The Transport Vehicles section of the Warhammer 40,000 rulebook explains how these dedicated transport vehicles work.

Options: This section lists all of the upgrades you may add to the unit if you wish to do so alongside the associated points cost for each. Where an option states that you may exchange one weapon 'and/or' another, you may replace either, neither or both provided you pay the points cost.

CHARACTERS AND OTHER REGIMENTS

You'll notice that the named characters in the Imperial Guard army list are drawn from several different regiments, but they can still be used in the same army if you wish. This can represent the common occurance of different Imperial Guard regiments fighting alongside on another. Alternatively, you can use the model and rules for a named character to represent a hero of a different regiment – for example, using the rules and model for Lord Castellan Creed as the Company Commander of your Mordian army, or a regiment of your own design – you just need to come up with a new name. This is a perfect way to personalise your army, just make sure that your opponent is aware of what every character in your army counts as.

STANDARD MISSIONS

COMPULSORY	OPTIONAL	OPTIONAL
1 HQ	1 HQ	3 Fast Attack
2 Troops	4 Troops	3 Heavy Support
	3 Elites	

HQ

COMPANY COMMAND SQUAD ....50 POINTS Page 30

	WS	BS	S	T	W	I	A	Ld	Sv
Company Commander	4	4	3	3	3	3	3	9	5+
Veteran	3	4	3	3	1	3	1	7	5+
Veteran Weapons Team	3	4	3	3	2	3	2	7	5+

Composition:
- Company Commander
- 4 Veterans

Unit Type:
- Infantry

Wargear:
- Flak armour
- Lasgun (Company Commander has a laspistol instead)
- Close-combat weapon
- Frag grenades
- The Company Commander also has a refractor field

Special Rules:
- Senior Officer (Company Commander only)

Transport:
- The squad may take a Chimera as a dedicated transport (see page 99 for points cost).

OPTIONS:
- The Company Commander may exchange his laspistol and/or close-combat weapon for:
  - Bolt pistol or boltgun ....2 points
  - Power weapon...10 points
  - Plasma pistol ....10 points
  - Power fist...15 points
- The Company Commander may have melta bombs...5 points
- Any Veteran may replace his lasgun with:
  - Laspistol ....free
- One Veteran may be upgraded to carry:
  - Medi-pack ....30 points
- One other Veteran may be upgraded to carry:
  - Regimental standard ....15 points
- One other Veteran may be upgraded to carry:
  - Vox-caster ....5 points
- One other Veteran may replace his lasgun with:
  - Heavy flamer..20 points
- Replace two other Veterans with a Veteran Weapons Team armed with one of the following:
  - Mortar ....5 points
  - Autocannon or heavy bolter..............................10 points
  - Missile launcher ....15 points
  - Lascannon..20 points
- Any remaining Veterans that have not been upgraded with one of the options above may replace their lasguns with:
  - Flamer, grenade launcher or sniper rifle..5 points per model
  - Meltagun ....10 points per model
  - Plasma gun ....15 points per model
- The entire squad (including any Regimental Advisors) may have any of the following:
  - Krak grenades...5 points
  - Carapace armour ....20 points
  - Camo cloaks ....20 points

Regimental Advisors
- The squad may be joined by any of the following:
  - One Astropath ....30 points
  - One Master of Ordnance ....30 points
  - One Officer of the Fleet ....30 points
  - Up to two Bodyguards ....15 points per model

	WS	BS	S	T	W	I	A	Ld	Sv
Astropath	3	4	3	3	1	3	1	7	5+
Master of Ordnance	3	4	3	3	1	3	1	7	5+
Officer of the Fleet	3	4	3	3	1	3	1	7	5+
Bodyguard	4	4	3	3	1	3	2	7	5+

ASTROPATH
Wargear:
- Flak armour
- Laspistol
- Close-combat weapon
- Frag grenades

Special Rules:
- Telepathic Relay

MASTER OF ORDNANCE
Wargear:
- Flak armour
- Laspistol
- Close-combat weapon
- Frag grenades

Special Rules:
- Artillery Bombardment

OFFICER OF THE FLEET
Wargear:
- Flak armour
- Laspistol
- Close-combat weapon
- Frag grenades

Special Rules:
- Intercept Reserves

BODYGUARD
Wargear:
- Flak armour
- Laspistol
- Close-combat weapon
- Frag grenades

Special Rules:
- Look out – Arghh!

HQ

LORD CASTELLAN CREED .... 90 points — Page 57
One Company Command Squad in your army may replace its Company Commander with Lord Castellan Creed.

	WS	BS	S	T	W	I	A	Ld	Sv
Ursarkar Creed	4	4	3	3	3	3	3	10	4+

Unit Type:
- Infantry (unique)

Wargear:
- Carapace armour
- Two hot-shot laspistols (fires as a twin-linked hot-shot laspistol)
- Frag grenades
- Refractor field

Special Rules:
- Supreme Commander
- Tactical Genius

COLOUR SERGEANT KELL .... 85 points — Page 57
One Company Command Squad in your army may replace a Veteran with Colour Sergeant Kell. No Veterans may be upgraded to carry a regimental standard in a Command Squad that includes Colour Sergeant Kell.

	WS	BS	S	T	W	I	A	Ld	Sv
Jarran Kell	4	4	3	3	2	4	2	8	4+

Unit Type:
- Infantry (unique)

Wargear:
- Carapace armour
- Laspistol
- Power weapon
- Power fist
- Frag grenades
- Regimental standard

Special Rules:
- Sworn Protector
- Listen up Maggots!

COLONEL 'IRON HAND' STRAKEN .... 95 points — Page 60
One Company Command Squad in your army may replace its Company Commander with Colonel 'Iron Hand' Straken.

	WS	BS	S	T	W	I	A	Ld	Sv
Colonel Straken	5	4	6	4	3	3	3	9	3+

Unit Type:
- Infantry (unique)

Wargear:
- Flak armour
- Plasma pistol
- Shotgun
- Close-combat weapon
- Frag grenades
- Refractor field

Special Rules:
- Gung-ho
- Senior Officer
- Cold Steel and Courage
- Man of Adamantium

NORK DEDDOG .... 110 points — Page 67
One Company Command Squad in your army may take Nork Deddog. If a Command Squad includes Nork Deddog it may not take any Bodyguards as Regimental Advisors.

	WS	BS	S	T	W	I	A	Ld	Sv
Nork Deddog	4	3	5	5	3	3	4	8	4+

Unit Type:
- Infantry (unique)

Wargear:
- Carapace armour
- Ripper gun
- Frag grenades

Special Rules:
- Feel No Pain
- Furious Charge
- Bulky
- Stubborn
- Loyal to the End
- Heroic Sacrifice

HQ

LORD COMMISSAR ....70 points Page 32

	WS	BS	S	T	W	I	A	Ld	Sv
Lord Commissar	5	5	3	3	3	3	3	10	5+

Composition:
- 1 Lord Commissar

Unit Type:
- Infantry

Wargear:
- Flak armour
- Bolt pistol
- Close-combat weapon
- Frag and krak grenades
- Refractor field

Special Rules:
- Independent Character
- Stubborn
- Summary Execution
- Aura of Discipline

OPTIONS:
- The Lord Commissar may exchange his bolt pistol and/or Close-combat weapon for:
  - Boltgun ....*free*
  - Power weapon ....*10 points*
  - Plasma pistol ....*10 points*
  - Power fist...*15 points*
- The Lord Commissar may take any of the following:
  - Carapace armour ....*10 points*
  - Camo cloak...*10 points*
  - Melta bombs...*5 points*

Transport:
- A Lord Commissar may take a Chimera as a dedicated transport (see page 99 for points cost).

COMMISSAR YARRICK ....**185 points** Page 63

	WS	BS	S	T	W	I	A	Ld	Sv
Commissar Yarrick	5	5	3	4	3	3	3	10	4+

Unit Type:
- Infantry (unique)

Wargear:
- Carapace armour
- Storm bolter
- Battle klaw (counts as a power fist)
- Close-combat weapon
- Bolt pistol
- Frag and krak grenades
- Force field
- Bale Eye

Special Rules:
- Independent Character
- Eternal Warrior
- Aura of Discipline
- Inspirational Hero
- Iron Will

Transport:
- Commissar Yarrick may take a Chimera as a dedicated transport (see page 99 for points cost).

PRIMARIS PSYKER ....**70 points** Page 33

	WS	BS	S	T	W	I	A	Ld	Sv
Primaris Psyker	4	4	3	3	2	3	3	9	5+

Composition:
- 1 Primaris Psyker

Unit Type:
- Infantry

Wargear:
- Flak armour
- Laspistol
- Force weapon
- Frag grenades
- Refractor field

Special Rules:
- Independent Character
- Psyker
- It's For Your Own Good

Psychic Powers:
- Lightning Arc
- Nightshroud

HQ

Page 35

MINISTORUM PRIEST ....45 points

An Imperial Guard army may include 0-5 Ministorum Priests. Priests do not use up any Force Organisation chart selections, but are otherwise treated as separate HQ units.

	WS	BS	S	T	W	I	A	Ld	Sv
Ministorum Priest	3	3	3	3	1	3	2	7	5+

Composition:
• Priest

Unit Type:
• Infantry

Wargear:
• Flak armour
• Laspistol
• Close-combat weapon
• Frag grenades
• Rosarius

Special Rules:
• Independent Character
• Righteous Fury

OPTIONS:
• The Priest may exchange his laspistol for:
  - Shotgun ....*free*
• The Priest may exchange his close-combat weapon for:
  - Eviscerator ....*15 points*

Page 34

TECHPRIEST ENGINSEER ....45 points

An Imperial Guard army may include 0-2 Techpriest Enginseers. Techpriest Enginseers do not use up any Force Organisation chart selections, but are otherwise treated as separate HQ units.

	WS	BS	S	T	W	I	A	Ld	Sv
Techpriest Enginseer	3	3	3	3	1	3	1	8	3+
Servitor	3	3	3	3	1	3	1	8	4+

Composition:
• 1 Techpriest

Unit Type:
• Infantry

Wargear (Techpriest):
• Power armour
• Laspistol
• Power weapon
• Servo-arm
• Frag and krak grenades

Wargear (Servitor):
• Servo-arm
• Carapace armour

Special Rules:
• Blessings of the Omnissiah
• Mindlock

OPTIONS:
• The Techpriest may take melta bombs ....*5 points*
• May be accompanied by up to five Servitors
  ....*15 points per model*
• Up to two Servitors may replace their servo-arm with:
  - A heavy bolter ....*20 points*
  - A multi-melta or plasma-cannon ....*30 points*

ELITES

OGRYN SQUAD .... 130 POINTS Page 42

	WS	BS	S	T	W	I	A	Ld	Sv
Ogryn	4	3	5	5	3	2	3	6	5+
Ogryn Bone 'ead	4	3	5	5	3	2	4	7	5+

Composition:
• 1 Ogryn
  Bone 'ead
• 2 Ogryns

Unit Type:
• Infantry

Wargear:
• Flak armour
• Ripper gun
• Frag grenades

Special Rules:
• Bulky
• Furious Charge
• Stubborn

OPTIONS:
• May have up to seven
  - additional Ogryns ....*40 points per model*

Transport:
• The squad may take a Chimera as a
  dedicated transport (see page 99 for
  points cost).

RATLING SQUAD .... 30 POINTS Page 43

	WS	BS	S	T	W	I	A	Ld	Sv
Ratling	2	4	2	2	1	4	1	6	5+

Composition:
• 3 Ratlings

Unit Type:
• Infantry

Wargear:
• Flak armour
• Sniper rifle
• Laspistol

Special Rules:
• Infiltrate
• Stealth

OPTIONS:
• May have up to seven
  - additional Ratlings ....*10 points per model*

PSYKER BATTLE SQUAD .... 60 POINTS Page 47

	WS	BS	S	T	W	I	A	Ld	Sv
Sanctioned Psyker	2	3	2	3	1	3	1	9	5+
Overseer	3	3	3	3	1	3	2	9	5+

Composition:
• 1 Overseer
• 4 Sanctioned
  Psykers

Unit Type:
• Infantry

Wargear:
• Flak armour
• Laspistol
• Close-combat weapon

Special Rules:
• Psyker (Sanctioned Psykers only)
• Psychic Choir
• Ultimate Sanction

Psychic Powers:
• Weaken Resolve
• Soulstorm

OPTIONS:
• May have up to five
  - additional Sanctioned Psykers ....*10 points per model*

Transport:
• The squad may take a Chimera as a
  dedicated transport (see page 99 for
  points cost).

ELITES

STORM TROOPER SQUAD ....85 POINTS   **Page 46**

	WS	BS	S	T	W	I	A	Ld	Sv
Storm Trooper	3	4	3	3	1	3	1	7	4+
Storm Trooper Sgt.	3	4	3	3	1	3	2	8	4+

Composition:
- 1 Storm Trooper Sergeant
- 4 Storm Troopers

Unit Type:
- Infantry

Wargear:
- Carapace armour
- Hot-shot lasgun
- Hot-shot laspistol
- Close-combat weapon
- Frag grenades
- Krak grenades

Special Rules:
- Deep Strike
- Special Operations

OPTIONS:
- May have up to five
  - additional Storm Troopers.................*16 points per model*
- The Storm Trooper Sergeant may exchange his hot-shot laspistol and/or hot-shot lasgun for:
  - Bolt pistol or boltgun...*free*
  - Power weapon...*10 points*
  - Plasma pistol ....*10 points*
- Up to two Storm Troopers may replace their hot-shot lasgun with:
  - Flamer...*5 points per model*
  - Grenade launcher...............................*5 points per model*
  - Meltagun ....*10 points per model*
  - Plasma gun ....*15 points per model*

Transport:
- The squad may take a Chimera as a dedicated transport (see page 99 for points cost).

GUARDSMAN MARBO ....65 points   **Page 61**

	WS	BS	S	T	W	I	A	Ld	Sv
Guardsman Marbo	5	5	3	3	2	5	4	7	5+

Unit Type:
- Infantry (unique)

Wargear:
- Flak armour
- Ripper pistol
- Envenomed blade
- Frag grenades
- Melta bombs
- Demolition charge

Special Rules:
- Fearless
- Stealth
- Move Through Cover
- Hit and Run
- Fleet
- Loner
- He's Behind You!

TROOPS

INFANTRY PLATOON

Composition: 1 Platoon Command Squad, 2-5 Infantry Squads, 0-5 Heavy Weapons Squads, 0-2 Special Weapons Squads and 0-1 Conscripts Squad. Each Infantry Platoon counts as a single Troops choice on the force organisation chart when deploying, and is rolled for collectively when rolling for reserves.

PLATOON COMMAND SQUAD* ....**30 Points**   **Page 36**

	WS	BS	S	T	W	I	A	Ld	Sv
Platoon Commander	4	4	3	3	1	3	2	8	5+
Guardsman	3	3	3	3	1	3	1	7	5+
Heavy Weapons Team	3	3	3	3	2	3	2	7	5+
Commissar	4	4	3	3	1	3	2	9	5+

Composition:
- 1 Platoon Commander
- 4 Guardsmen

Unit Type:
- Infantry

Transport:
- The squad may take a Chimera as a dedicated transport (see page 99 for points cost).

Wargear:
- Flak armour
- Lasgun (Platoon Commander has laspistol instead, Commissar has bolt pistol instead)
- Close-combat weapon
- Frag grenades

Special Rules:
- Junior Officer (Platoon Commander only)
- Stubborn (Commissar only)
- Summary Execution (Commissar only)

OPTIONS:
- The Platoon Commander may exchange his laspistol for:
  - Bolt pistol ....*2 points*
- A Platoon Commander may take melta bombs ......*5 points*
- The squad may be joined by a Commissar............*35 points*
- The Platoon Commander and/or Commissar may exchange his pistol and/or close-combat weapon for:
  - Boltgun...*2 points*
  - Power weapon...*10 points*
  - Plasma pistol ....*10 points*
  - Power fist...*15 points*
- Any Guardsman may replace his lasgun with:
  - Laspistol ....*free*
- One Guardsman may have:
  - Medi-pack ....*30 points*
- One other Guardsman may have:
  - Platoon standard ....*15 points*
- One other Guardsman may have:
  - Vox-caster ....*5 points*
- One other Guardsman may replace his lasgun with:
  - Heavy flamer..*20 points*
- Replace two other Guardsmen with a Heavy Weapons Team armed with one of the following:
  - Mortar ....*5 points*
  - Autocannon or heavy bolter.............................*10 points*
  - Missile launcher ....*15 points*
  - Lascannon..*20 points*
- Any remaining Guardsman that has not been upgraded with one of the options above may replace his lasgun with:
  - Flamer, grenade launcher or sniper rifle..*5 points per model*
  - Meltagun ....*10 points per model*
  - Plasma gun ....*15 points per model*
- The entire squad may have krak grenades..............*5 points*

COMMANDER CHENKOV....................................**50 points**   **Page 65**
One Platoon Command Squad in your army may replace its Platoon Commander with Commander Chenkov.

	WS	BS	S	T	W	I	A	Ld	Sv
Commander Chenkov	4	4	3	3	2	3	2	9	4+

Unit Type:
- Infantry (unique)

Wargear:
- Carapace armour
- Power weapon
- Frag grenades
- Bolt pistol

Special Rules:
- Taskmaster
- Forward, You Dogs!
- Send in the Next Wave

CAPTAIN AL'RAHEM....................................**70 points**   **Page 64**
One Platoon Command Squad in your army may replace its Platoon Commander with Captain Al'rahem.

	WS	BS	S	T	W	I	A	Ld	Sv
Captain Al'rahem	4	4	3	3	2	3	2	9	5+

Unit Type:
- Infantry (unique)

Wargear:
- Flak armour
- Plasma pistol
- Frag grenades
- Claw of the Desert Tigers

Special Rules:
- Stalk the Enemy
- Desert Raider

TROOPS

INFANTRY SQUAD* ....50 Points   **Page 37**

	WS	BS	S	T	W	I	A	Ld	Sv
Guardsman	3	3	3	3	1	3	1	7	5+
Sergeant	3	3	3	3	1	3	2	8	5+
Heavy Weapons Team	3	3	3	3	2	3	2	7	5+
Commissar	4	4	3	3	1	3	2	9	5+

Composition:
- 1 Sergeant
- 9 Guardsmen

Unit Type:
- Infantry

Transport:
- The squad may take a Chimera as a dedicated transport (see page 99 for points cost).

Wargear:
- Flak armour
- Lasgun
  (Sergeant has laspistol instead, Commissar has bolt pistol instead)
- Close-combat weapon
- Frag grenades

Special Rules:
- Combined Squad
- Stubborn (Commissar only)
- Summary Execution (Commissar only)

OPTIONS:
- The Sergeant may exchange his laspistol for:
  - Bolt pistol ....*2 points*
- The Sergeant may take melta bombs.................*5 points*
- The squad may be joined by a Commissar...........*35 points*
- The Sergeant and/or Commissar may exchange his pistol and/or close-combat weapon for:
  - Power weapon or plasma pistol ....*10 points*
- One Guardsman may replace his lasgun with a:
  - Flamer, grenade launcher or sniper rifle...............*5 points*
  - Meltagun ....*10 points*
  - Plasma gun ....*15 points*
- One other Guardsman may have:
  - Vox-caster ....*5 points*
- Replace two Guardsmen with a Heavy Weapons Team armed with one of the following:
  - Mortar ....*5 points*
  - Autocannon or heavy bolter...........................*10 points*
  - Missile launcher ....*15 points*
  - Lascannon...*20 points*
- The entire squad may have krak grenades...........*10 points*

HEAVY WEAPONS SQUAD* ....60 Points   **Page 38**

	WS	BS	S	T	W	I	A	Ld	Sv
Heavy Weapons Team	3	3	3	3	2	3	2	7	5+

Composition:
- 3 Heavy Weapons Teams

Unit Type:
- Infantry

Wargear:
- Flak armour
- Lasgun
- Mortar
- Close-combat weapon
- Frag grenades

OPTIONS:
- Any Heavy Weapons Team may exchange its mortar for a:
  - Heavy bolter or autocannon ....*5 points*
  - Missile launcher ....*10 points*
  - Lascannon...*15 points*
- The entire squad may have krak grenades..............*5 points*

SPECIAL WEAPONS SQUAD* ....35 Points   **Page 38**

	WS	BS	S	T	W	I	A	Ld	Sv
Guardsman	3	3	3	3	1	3	1	7	5+

Composition:
- 6 Guardsmen

Unit Type:
- Infantry

Wargear:
- Flak armour
- Lasgun
- Close-combat weapon

OPTIONS:
- Three Guardsmen must choose one of the following options:
  - replace his lasgun with a flamer, grenade launcher or sniper rifle...........................*5 points*
  - replace his lasgun with a meltagun ....*10 points*
  - replace his lasgun with a plasma gun.................*15 points*
  - take a demolition charge ....*20 points*

CONSCRIPTS* ....80 Points   **Page 37**

	WS	BS	S	T	W	I	A	Ld	Sv
Conscript	2	2	3	3	1	3	1	5	5+

Composition:
- 20 Conscripts

Unit Type:
- Infantry

Wargear:
- Flak armour
- Lasgun
- Close-combat weapon

OPTIONS:
- May include up to an additional 30 conscripts
  ....*4 points per model*
- If your army includes Commander Chenkov, any unit of Conscripts may be given the Send in the Next Wave special rule ....*75 points*

Note that the units on these two pages may not be chosen individually – only as part of an Infantry Platoon.

TROOPS

VETERAN SQUAD ....70 POINTS

Page 40

	WS	BS	S	T	W	I	A	Ld	Sv
Veteran	3	4	3	3	1	3	1	7	5+
Veteran Sergeant	3	4	3	3	1	3	2	8	5+
Veteran Weapons Team	3	4	3	3	2	3	2	7	5+

Composition:
- 1 Veteran Sergeant
- 9 Veterans

Unit Type:
- Infantry

Wargear:
- Flak armour
- Lasgun (Veteran Sergeant has laspistol instead)
- Close-combat weapon
- Frag and krak grenades

Transport:
- The squad may take a Chimera as a dedicated transport (see page 99 for points cost).

OPTIONS:
- The Veteran Sergeant may exchange his laspistol and/or Close-combat weapon for:
  - Shotgun ....*free*
  - Bolt pistol ....*2 points*
  - Power weapon...*10 points*
  - Plasma pistol ....*10 points*
  - Power fist...*15 points*
- Any Veteran may replace his lasgun with a shotgun .....*free*
- One Veteran may have:
  - Vox-caster ....*5 points*
- Up to three other Veterans may replace their lasguns with:
  - Flamer, grenade launcher or sniper rifle...............*5 points*
  - Meltagun ....*10 points*
  - Plasma gun ....*15 points*
  - Heavy flamer (one per squad)............................*20 points*
- Replace two Veterans with a Veteran Weapons Team armed with one of the following:
  - Mortar ....*5 points*
  - Autocannon or heavy bolter............................*10 points*
  - Missile launcher ....*15 points*
  - Lascannon...*20 points*
- The squad can choose any of the following doctrines:
  - *Grenadiers:* The squad replaces its flak armour with carapace armour ....*30 points*
  - *Forward Sentries:* The squad has camo-cloaks and snare mines..*30 points*
  - *Demolitions:* The entire squad has melta bombs. One Veteran carries a demolition charge in addition to his other equipment..*30 points*

GUNNERY SERGEANT HARKER ....55 Points

Page 62

One Veteran squad in your army may replace its Veteran Sergeant with Gunnery Sergeant 'Stonetooth' Harker.
If a squad includes Gunnery Sergeant Harker it may not take the Grenadiers doctrine.

	WS	BS	S	T	W	I	A	Ld	Sv
Gunnery Sgt. Harker	4	4	4	3	1	3	2	8	5+

Unit Type:
- Infantry (unique)

Wargear:
- Flak armour
- Close-combat weapon
- Frag and krak grenades
- 'Payback' (heavy bolter)

Special Rules:
- Relentless
- Feel No Pain
- Catachan Devils

SERGEANT BASTONNE ....60 Points

Page 59

One Veteran squad in your army may replace its Veteran Sergeant with Sergeant Lukas Bastonne.

	WS	BS	S	T	W	I	A	Ld	Sv
Lukas Bastonne	4	4	3	3	1	3	2	10	4+

Unit Type:
- Infantry (unique)

Wargear:
- Carapace armour
- Hot-shot laspistol
- Frag and krak grenades
- Power sword

Special Rules:
- It's Up to us, Lads
- Never Give Up, Never Surrender!

TROOPS

PENAL LEGION SQUAD .... 80 POINTS — Page 41

	WS	BS	S	T	W	I	A	Ld	Sv
Penal Legionnaire	3	3	3	3	1	3	1	8	5+
Penal Custodian	3	3	3	3	1	3	2	8	5+

Composition:
- 1 Custodian
- 9 Penal Legionnaires

Unit Type:
- Infantry

Wargear:
- Flak armour
- Lasgun (Penal Custodian has laspistol instead)
- Close-combat weapon

Special Rules:
- Desperadoes
- Scouts
- Stubborn

Schaeffer's Last Chancers

Amongst the Imperium's many penal legions is one that stands out above the rest – the 13th Penal Legion, also known as the Last Chancers. Led by the fiercely uncompromising Colonel Schaeffer, this unit is the last stop for the worst scum in the galaxy. Schaeffer's ethos is simple; he will give the troops in his charge one last chance to win the Emperor's forgiveness and in so doing save their souls. He will give them this chance by leading them into the most perilous warzones to perform the most suicidal missions imaginable. Such is the Colonel's reputation that many of those offered the chance to join the Last Chancers choose death rather than follow him.

DEDICATED TRANSPORTS

Many Imperial Guard units have the option of selecting a dedicated transport vehicle. These vehicles do not use up any force organisation chart selections, but otherwise function as separate units. See the Vehicles section of the Warhammer 40,000 rulebook for details of how transport vehicles operate.

CHIMERA ARMOURED TRANSPORT .... 55 POINTS — Page 39

		⌐ Armour ⌐		
	BS	F	S	R
Chimera	3	12	10	10

Composition:
- 1 Chimera

Unit Type:
- Vehicle (tank)

Wargear:
- Multi-laser
- Heavy bolter
- Searchlight
- Smoke Launchers

Special Rules:
- Amphibious
- Mobile Command Vehicle

Transport Capacity:
12 models

OPTIONS:
- Replace multi-laser with:
  - Heavy flamer or heavy bolter .... *free*
- Replace heavy bolter with:
  - Heavy flamer .... *free*
- Take any of the following:
  - Pintle-mounted storm bolter or heavy stubber . *10 points*
  - Hunter-killer missile .... *10 points*
  - Dozer blade .... *10 points*
  - Extra armour .... *15 points*
  - Camo netting .... *20 points*

FAST ATTACK

SCOUT SENTINEL SQUADRON .... 35 POINTS PER MODEL   Page 45

	WS	BS	S	Armour F	Armour S	Armour R	I	A
Scout Sentinel	3	3	5	10	10	10	3	1

Composition:
- Vehicle squadron of 1-3 Scout Sentinels

Unit Type:
- Vehicle (walker, open topped)

Wargear:
- Multi-laser

Special Rules:
- Scouts
- Move Through Cover

OPTIONS:
- Any Sentinel may replace its multi-laser with one of the following weapons:
  - Heavy flamer or autocannon .... 5 points per model
  - Missile launcher .... 10 points per model
  - Lascannon .... 15 points per model
- Any model may take any of the following:
  - Searchlight .... 1 point per model
  - Hunter-killer missile .... 10 points per model
- The entire squadron may take:
  - Smoke launchers .... 5 points per model
  - Camo netting .... 10 points per model

ARMOURED SENTINEL SQUADRON .... 55 POINTS PER MODEL   Page 45

	WS	BS	S	Armour F	Armour S	Armour R	I	A
Armoured Sentinel	3	3	5	12	10	10	3	1

Composition:
- Vehicle squadron of 1-3 Armoured Sentinels

Unit Type:
- Vehicle (walker)

Wargear:
- Multi-laser
- Extra Armour

OPTIONS:
- Any Sentinel may replace its multi-laser with one of the following weapons:
  - Heavy flamer or autocannon .... 5 points per model
  - Missile launcher .... 10 points per model
  - Lascannon .... 15 points per model
  - Plasma cannon .... 20 points per model
- Any model may take any of the following:
  - Searchlight .... 1 point per model
  - Hunter-killer missile .... 10 points per model
- The entire squadron may take:
  - Smoke launchers .... 5 points per model
  - Camo netting .... 10 points per model

ROUGH RIDER SQUAD .... 55 POINTS   Page 44

	WS	BS	S	T	W	I	A	Ld	Sv
Rough Rider	3	3	3	3	1	3	1	7	5+
Rough Rider Sergeant	3	3	3	3	1	3	2	8	5+

Composition:
- 1 Rough Rider Sergeant
- 4 Rough Riders

Unit Type:
- Cavalry

Wargear:
- Flak armour
- Hunting lance
- Laspistol or close-combat weapon
- Frag grenades
- Krak grenades

OPTIONS:
- May have up to five additional Rough Riders
  .... 10 points per model
- The Rough Rider Sergeant may exchange his laspistol for:
  - Power weapon .... 10 points
  - Plasma pistol .... 10 points
- The Rough Rider Sergeant may take melta bombs .. 5 points
- Up to two Rough Riders may replace their hunting lance with one of the following:
  - Flamer or grenade launcher .... 5 points per model
  - Meltagun .... 10 points per model
  - Plasma gun .... 15 points per model

MOGUL KAMIR .... 40 Points   Page 66

One Rough Rider squad in your army may replace its Rough Rider sergeant with Mogul Kamir.

	WS	BS	S	T	W	I	A	Ld	Sv
Mogul Kamir	4	3	3	3	2	3	3	8	5+

Unit Type:
- Cavalry (unique)

Wargear:
- Flak armour
- Hunting lance
- Cyber-steed
- Bolt pistol
- Close-combat weapon
- Frag grenades
- Krak grenades

Special Rules:
- Khanasan's Fiercest
- Vicious Temperament

FAST ATTACK

Page 50

HELLHOUND SQUADRON

Composition: Vehicle squadron composed of 1-3 of the following tanks, in any combination:

Hellhound ....130 POINTS PER MODEL

Devil Dog ....120 POINTS PER MODEL

Bane Wolf ....130 POINTS PER MODEL

		Armour		
	BS	F	S	R
Hellhound	3	12	12	10
Devil Dog	3	12	12	10
Bane Wolf	3	12	12	10

Unit Type:
- Vehicle (tank, fast)

Wargear (All):
- Heavy bolter

Wargear Hellhound:
- Inferno cannon

Devil Dog:
- Melta cannon

Bane Wolf:
- Chem cannon

OPTIONS:
- Any model may replace heavy bolter with:
  - Heavy flamer ....*free*
  - Multi-melta ....*15 points per model*
- Any model may take any of the following:
  - Searchlight ....*1 point per model*
  - Pintle-mounted storm bolter or heavy stubber
  ....*10 points per model*
  - Hunter-killer missile ....*10 points per model*
  - Dozer blade.........................*10 points per model*
  - Extra armour ....*15 points per model*
- The entire squadron may take:
  - Smoke launchers ....*5 points per model*
  - Camo netting....................*20 points per model*

VALKYRIE ASSAULT CARRIER SQUADRON ....100 POINTS PER MODEL

Page 56

		Armour		
	BS	F	S	R
Valkyrie	3	12	12	10

Composition:
- Vehicle squadron of 1-3 Valkyries

Unit Type:
- Vehicle (fast, skimmer)

Transport Capacity:
12 models

Wargear:
- Multi-laser
- 2 Hellstrike Missiles
- Searchlight
- Extra Armour

Special Rules:
- Deep Strike
- Scout
- Grav Chute Insertion

OPTIONS:
- Any Valkyrie may replace its multi-laser with:
  - Lascannon........................*15 points per model*
- Any Valkyrie may exchange both of its hellstrike missiles for:
  - Two multiple rocket pods ....*30 points per model*
- Any Valkyrie may take a pair of sponsons armed with:
  - Heavy bolters ....*10 points per model*

VENDETTA GUNSHIP SQUADRON ....130 POINTS PER MODEL

Page 56

		Armour		
	BS	F	S	R
Vendetta	3	12	12	10

Composition:
- Vehicle squadron of 1-3 Vendettas

Unit Type:
- Vehicle (fast, skimmer)

Transport Capacity:
12 models

Wargear:
- 3 twin-linked lascannons
- Searchlight
- Extra Armour

Special Rules:
- Deep Strike
- Scout
- Grav Chute Insertion

OPTIONS:
- Any Vendetta may exchange two twin-linked lascannons for:
  - Two hellfury missiles ....*free*
- Any Vendetta may take a pair of sponsons armed with:
  - Heavy bolters ....*10 points per model*

HEAVY SUPPORT

LEMAN RUSS SQUADRON

Page 48

Composition: Vehicle squadron composed of 1-3 of the following tanks, in any combination:

Leman Russ Battle Tank..........150 POINTS PER MODEL
Leman Russ Exterminator..150 POINTS PER MODEL
Leman Russ Vanquisher..........155 POINTS PER MODEL
Leman Russ Eradicator............160 POINTS PER MODEL
Leman Russ Demolisher........165 POINTS PER MODEL
Leman Russ Punisher..............180 POINTS PER MODEL
Leman Russ Executioner.......190 POINTS PER MODEL

	BS	F	S	R
		Armour		
Leman Russ Battle Tank	3	14	13	10
Leman Russ Exterminator	3	14	13	10
Leman Russ Vanquisher	3	14	13	10
Leman Russ Eradicator	3	14	13	10
Leman Russ Demolisher	3	14	13	11
Leman Russ Punisher	3	14	13	11
Leman Russ Executioner	3	14	13	11

Unit Type:
• Vehicle (tank)

Wargear (All):
• Heavy bolter
• Searchlight
• Smoke launchers

Special Rules:
• Lumbering Behemoth

Wargear
Leman Russ:
• Battle cannon

Leman Russ Exterminator:
• Exterminator autocannon

Leman Russ Vanquisher:
• Vanquisher battle cannon

Leman Russ Eradicator:
• Eradicator nova cannon

Leman Russ Demolisher:
• Demolisher siege cannon

Leman Russ Punisher
• Punisher gatling cannon

Leman Russ Executioner
• Executioner plasma cannon

OPTIONS:
• Any model may exchange its heavy bolter for:
  - Heavy flamer ....*free*
  - Lascannon ....*15 points per model*
• Any model may take a pair of sponsons armed with
  - Heavy bolters or heavy flamers ....*20 points per model*
  - Multi-meltas ....*30 points per model*
  - Plasma cannons................................*40 points per model*
• Any model may take any of the following:
  - Pintle-mounted storm bolter or heavy stubber
  ....*10 points per model*
  - Hunter-killer missile ....*10 points per model*
  - Dozer blade......................................*10 points per model*
  - Extra armour ....*15 points per model*
• The entire squadron may take:
  - Camo netting....................................*20 points per model*

KNIGHT COMMANDER PASK ....*50 Points*

Page 58

**A single model in a Leman Russ squadron may take Knight Commander Pask as an upgrade.
You may only include one Knight Commander Pask in your army.**

Special Rules:
• Leman Russ Tank Ace
• Crack Shot

HYDRA FLAK TANK BATTERY ....*75 POINTS PER MODEL*

Page 51

Composition: Vehicle squadron composed of 1-3 Hydra Flak tanks.

	BS	F	S	R
		Armour		
Hydra	3	12	10	10

Unit Type:
• Vehicle (tank)

Wargear:
• Two twin-linked Hydra autocannons
• Heavy bolter
• Searchlight
• Smoke launchers
• Auto-targeting System

OPTIONS:
• Any model may replace its heavy bolter with:
  - Heavy flamer ....*free*
• Any model may take any of the following:
  - Pintle-mounted storm bolter or heavy stubber
  ....*10 points per model*
  - Hunter-killer missile ....*10 points per model*
  - Dozer blade......................................*10 points per model*
  - Extra armour ....*15 points per model*
• The entire squadron may take:
  - Camo netting....................................*20 points per model*

HEAVY SUPPORT

ORDNANCE BATTERY

Page 52

Composition: Vehicle squadron composed of 1-3 of the following tanks, in any combination:

Basilisk ....125 POINTS PER MODEL

Medusa ....135 POINTS PER MODEL

Colossus ....140 POINTS PER MODEL

Griffon ....75 POINTS PER MODEL

		Armour		
	BS	F	S	R
Basilisk	3	12	10	10
Medusa	3	12	10	10
Colossus	3	12	10	10
Griffon	3	12	10	10

Unit Type:
- Vehicle (tank, open-topped)

Wargear (All):
- Heavy bolter
- Searchlight
- Smoke launchers

Wargear

Basilisk:
- Earthshaker cannon

Medusa:
- Medusa siege cannon

Colossus:
- Colossus siege mortar

Griffon:
- Griffon heavy mortar

Special Rules:
- Accurate Bombardment (Griffon only)

OPTIONS:
- Any model may replace its heavy bolter with:
  - Heavy flamer ....*free*
- Any model may take any of the following:
  - Enclosed crew compartment ....*15 points per model*
  - Pintle-mounted storm bolter or heavy stubber
  ....*10 points per model*
  - Hunter-killer missile ....*10 points per model*
  - Dozer blade...........................*10 points per model*
  - Extra armour ....*15 points per model*
- The entire squadron may take:
  - Camo netting.....................................*30 points per model*
- Any Medusa may take bastion-breacher shells
  ....*5 points per model*

MANTICORE ROCKET LAUNCHER ....160 POINTS

Page 54

		Armour		
	BS	F	S	R
Manticore	3	12	10	10

Composition:
- 1 Manticore

Unit Type:
- Vehicle (tank)

Wargear:
- Storm eagle rockets
- Heavy bolter
- Searchlight
- Smoke launchers

Special Rules:
- Limited Ammunition

OPTIONS:
- Any model may replace its heavy bolter with:
  - Heavy flamer ....*free*
- Any model may take any of the following:
  - Pintle-mounted storm bolter or heavy stubber ...*10 points*
  - Hunter-killer missile ....*10 points*
  - Dozer blade ....*10 points*
  - Extra armour ....*15 points*
  - Camo netting..*30 points*

DEATHSTRIKE MISSILE LAUNCHER ....160 POINTS

Page 55

		Armour		
	BS	F	S	R
Deathstrike	3	12	12	10

Composition:
- 1 Deathstrike

Unit Type:
- Vehicle (tank)

Wargear:
- Deathstrike missile
- Heavy bolter
- Searchlight
- Smoke launchers

Special Rules:
- T-minus five minutes to launch...and counting

OPTIONS:
- Any model may replace its heavy bolter with:
  - Heavy flamer ....*free*
- Any model may take any of the following:
  - Pintle-mounted storm bolter or heavy stubber ...*10 points*
  - Hunter-killer missile ....*10 points*
  - Dozer blade ....*10 points*
  - Extra armour ....*15 points*
  - Camo netting..*30 points*

SUMMARY

TROOP TYPES

	WS	BS	S	T	W	I	A	Ld	Sv	Page
Astropath	3	4	3	3	1	3	1	7	5+	31
Bodyguard	4	4	3	3	1	3	2	7	5+	31
Captain Al'rahem	4	4	3	3	2	3	2	9	5+	64
Colonel Straken	5	4	6	4	3	3	3	9	3+	60
Commander Chenkov	4	4	3	3	2	3	2	9	4+	65
Commissar	4	4	3	3	1	3	2	9	5+	32
Commissar Yarrick	5	5	3	4	3	3	3	10	4+	63
Company Commander	4	4	3	3	3	3	3	9	5+	30
Conscript	2	2	3	3	1	3	1	5	5+	37
Guardsman Marbo	5	5	3	3	2	5	4	7	5+	61
Guardsman	3	3	3	3	1	3	1	7	5+	37
Gunnery Sergeant Harker	4	4	4	3	1	3	2	8	5+	62
Heavy Weapons Team	3	3	3	3	2	3	2	7	5+	38
Jarran Kell	4	4	3	3	2	4	2	8	4+	57
Lord Commissar	5	5	3	3	3	3	3	10	5+	32
Lukas Bastonne	4	4	3	3	1	3	2	10	4+	59
Master of Ordnance	3	4	3	3	1	3	1	7	5+	31
Ministorum Priest	3	3	3	3	1	3	2	7	5+	35
Mogul Kamir	4	3	3	3	2	3	3	8	5+	66
Nork Deddog	4	3	5	5	3	3	4	8	4+	67
Ogryn	4	3	5	5	3	2	3	6	5+	42
Ogryn Bone 'ead	4	3	5	5	3	2	4	7	5+	42
Officer of the Fleet	3	4	3	3	1	3	1	7	5+	31
Overseer	3	3	3	3	1	3	2	9	5+	47
Penal Custodian	3	3	3	3	1	3	2	8	5+	41
Penal Legionnaire	3	3	3	3	1	3	1	8	5+	41
Platoon Commander	4	4	3	3	1	3	2	8	5+	36
Primaris Psyker	4	4	3	3	2	3	3	9	5+	33
Ratling	2	4	2	2	1	4	1	6	5+	43
Rough Rider	3	3	3	3	1	3	1	7	5+	44
Rough Rider Sergeant	3	3	3	3	1	3	2	8	5+	44
Sanctioned Psyker	2	3	2	3	1	3	1	9	5+	47
Sergeant	3	3	3	3	1	3	2	8	5+	37
Servitor	3	3	3	3	1	3	1	8	4+	34
Storm Trooper	3	4	3	3	1	3	1	7	4+	46
Storm Trooper Sergeant	3	4	3	3	1	3	2	8	4+	46
Techpriest Enginseer	3	3	3	3	1	3	1	8	3+	34
Ursarkar Creed	4	4	3	3	3	3	3	10	4+	57
Veteran	3	4	3	3	1	3	1	7	5+	40
Veteran Sergeant	3	4	3	3	1	3	2	8	5+	40
Veteran Weapons Team	3	4	3	3	2	3	2	7	5+	40

VEHICLES

	BS	Armour Front	Side	Rear	Page
Bane Wolf	3	12	12	10	50
Basilisk	3	12	10	10	52
Chimera	3	12	10	10	39
Colossus	3	12	10	10	52
Deathstrike	3	12	12	10	55
Devil Dog	3	12	12	10	50
Griffon	3	12	10	10	52
Hellhound	3	12	12	10	50
Hydra	3	12	10	10	51
Leman Russ Battle Tank	3	14	13	10	48
Leman Russ Demolisher	3	14	13	11	48
Leman Russ Eradicator	3	14	13	10	48
Leman Russ Executioner	3	14	13	11	48
Leman Russ Exterminator	3	14	13	10	48
Leman Russ Punisher	3	14	13	11	48
Leman Russ Vanquisher	3	14	13	10	48
Manticore	3	12	10	10	54
Medusa	3	12	10	10	52
Valkyrie	3	12	12	10	56
Vendetta	3	12	12	10	56

	WS	BS	S	Armour Front	Side	Rear	I	A	Page
Armoured Sentinel	3	3	5	12	10	10	3	1	45
Scout Sentinel	3	3	5	10	10	10	3	1	45

WEAPON TYPES

Weapon	Range	Str.	AP	Type	
Autocannon	48"	7	4	Heavy 2	68
Bastion-breacher Shells	48"	10	1	Heavy 1, Blast*	53
Boltgun	24"	4	5	Rapid Fire	68
Bolt Pistol	12"	4	5	Pistol	68
Chem Cannon	Template	1	3	Heavy 1, Poisoned (2+)*	50
Demolition Charge	6"	8	2	Assault 1, Large Blast, One Shot Only	68
Eradicator Nova Cannon	36"	6	4	Heavy 1, Large Blast*	49
Executioner Plasma Cannon	36"	7	2	Heavy 3, Blast	49
Exterminator Autocannon	48"	7	4	Heavy 4, Twin-linked	49
Flamer	Template	4	5	Assault 1	68
Grenade Launcher*					68
(Frag)	24"	3	6	Assault 1, Blast	
(Krak)	24"	6	4	Assault 1	
Heavy Bolter	36"	5	4	Heavy 3	68
Heavy Flamer	Template	5	4	Assault 1	68
Heavy Stubber	36"	4	6	Heavy 3	70
Hellfury Missiles	72"	4	5	Heavy 1, Large Blast One Shot Only*	56
Hot-shot Lasgun	18"	3	3	Rapid Fire	46
Hot-shot Laspistol	6"	3	3	Pistol	68
Hydra Autocannon	72"	7	4	Heavy 2	51
Inferno Cannon	Template*	6	4	Heavy 1	50
Lascannon	48"	9	2	Heavy 1	69
Lasgun	24"	3	-	Rapid Fire	69
Laspistol	12"	3	-	Pistol	69
Meltagun	12"	8	1	Assault 1, Melta	69
Melta Cannon	24"	8	1	Heavy 1, Melta, Blast	50
Missile Launcher*					69
(Frag)	48"	4	6	Heavy 1, Blast	
(Krak)	48"	8	3	Heavy 1	
Mortar	48"	4	6	Heavy 1, Blast, Barrage	69
Multi-laser	36"	6	6	Heavy 3	70
Multi-melta	24"	8	1	Heavy 1, Melta	69
Multiple Rocket Pod	24"	4	6	Heavy 1, Large Blast	56
Plasma Cannon	36"	7	2	Heavy 1, Blast, Gets Hot!	69
Plasma Gun	24"	7	2	Rapid Fire, Gets Hot!	69
Plasma Pistol	12"	7	2	Pistol, Gets Hot!	69
Punisher Gatling Cannon	24"	5	-	Heavy 20	49
Ripper Gun	12"	5	-	Assault 3	42
Ripper Pistol	12"	X	2	Pistol, Sniper	61
Shotgun	12"	3	-	Assault 2	69
Sniper Rifle	36"	X	6	Heavy 1, Sniper	69
Storm Bolter	24"	4	5	Assault 2	71
Vanquisher Battle Cannon	72"	8	2	Heavy 1*	49

ORDNANCE

Weapon	Range	Str.	AP	Type	
Battle Cannon	72"	8	3	Ordnance 1, Large Blast	48
Colossus Siege Mortar	24"-240"	6	3	Ordnance Barrage 1, Large Blast*	53
Deathstrike Missile	12"-Unlimited	10	1	Ordnance Barrage, D3+3" Blast, One Shot Only*	55
Demolisher Siege Cannon	24"	10	2	Ordnance 1, Large Blast	49
Earthshaker Cannon	36"-240"	9	3	Ordnance Barrage 1, Large Blast	53
Griffon Heavy Mortar	12"-48"	6	4	Ordnance Barrage 1, Large Blast*	53
Hellstrike Missiles	72"	8	3	Ordnance 1, One Shot Only	56
Medusa Siege Cannon	36"	10	2	Ordnance 1, Large Blast	53
Storm Eagle Rockets	24"-120"	10	4	Ordnance Barrage D3*, Large Blast	54

*These weapons have additional rules as detailed in their entries.